He Must Increase

I *Must* Decrease

Terry Powell

Contents

Dedication

This book is dedicated to my grandchildren, Parks, Philip, and John, and others to come, maybe; and to your grandchildren, all of them so innocent and unsuspecting, all too soon to be severely challenged by the complexities of life; but more specifically, by the evil that lives among us; and if we are not wise and vigilant, within us.

Young people are generally naïve concerning the subtle and seductive nature of evil, its origin, its strategies, its horrors and the detestable fate it brings. Children must be taught. It is our greatest responsibility as adults. Our children do not learn much from what we say; they do learn from what we do. That is why it is so hard to teach children. If we live a lie, they will live it too.

• • •

Preface

Here I am, writing a Christian book for the first time. I have already assaulted the writing profession and the secular public, so why not now the religious folk. I have no credentials, except one. I am a Christian. Jesus said, "let the little children come unto me," so, here I am—childlike, trusting, loyal, and dependent. Doesn't really sound like credentials, does it? He said His Grace would be sufficient.

Maybe I have no business writing any book, Christian or otherwise. I am by nature and training a poor excuse for a scholar, a confession which would release a load of guilt from the stubborn hearts of many so-called scholars today.

Generally, I have more respect for the old scholars, who if they err, err on the side of caution. I am cautiously skeptical of the new ones. I often wonder if the primary qualification for modern scholarship is a worship of the human intellect, particularly one's own. Modern scholarship also seems to demand an affection for the security of tenure, the comfort of the great ideological think tank, the popularity of survey psychology, and the prideful intolerance for anyone who does not embrace your personal world view; and lest we forget, an overwhelming allegiance to relativism.

Since I am no scholar, I am automatically disqualified as a theologian. I have never met one in person so I cannot attest to what one would look like. But contrary to the masses, I can and do read what they write which makes me fairly familiar with what they sound like. They sound like they know more than they really know. Many of the theologians I have read consistently avoid answering my questions. They offer multiple choice speculations, or play word games with what I already know. I am nearly convinced that their theories and opinions are not much better than ours.

Modern day theologians, particularly the liberal ones, often ramble on and on and march a copyrighted circle around their favorite issue while singing the same verse thirty-nine times. Some dance around like politicians, drinking the new wine of political correctness, succeeding only in convincing us that politics is their true ambition. Rather than save mankind, they prefer to govern it. Their opinions are generally inconclusive and noncommittal and serve well to buy a little time for the devil. Jesus referred to them as "wolves in sheep's clothing."

And I have noticed that some of the more liberal ones cozy up to the devil and become his accomplices. Oops! I should not have mentioned the devil and liberalism in the same sentence. Now I have gone and done it. I have offended the many modern day theologians who do not believe the devil exists.

Do not expect an apology. What I really am by nature is a rebel. And the worst kind of rebel—a brazen fundamental Christian rebel who takes the Bible at face value and believes that the Spirit within me will not allow me to misinterpret it, or wander to the left or the right.

I will be happy to trade you my three thousand pages of titillating liberal theology for an old dog eared copy of Mother Goose; and I will trade you a congregation of modern day theologians for a righteous grandmother to read it to me. But, do not get me wrong, my measly opinion of scholars and theologians is of far less value than their scholarly efforts. Despite their defects and deficiencies, we need scholars and theologians; maybe not as much as we need plumbers; but they, like plumbers, poke and prod and help us to separate things out, and clear the air, and keep things moving along slowly and gradually.

Still, it is hard to have patience with them. They are always an aggravation and a costly inconvenience when you need one, whether it be a scholar, a theologian, or a plumber. It is clear to me that Jesus prefers plumbers.

• • •

"Who Do the People say I am?"

MATTHEW 16:13

"Who do the people say I am?"

MATTHEW 16:13

Chapter 1

It was Thursday night, His last night. Jesus knew he would be murdered on Friday. The three and a half years assigned to His public ministry had expired. Only hours stood between Him and the horrors of the cross. There would be no sleep this night, no rest, hardly a breath without the taunting roars of Satan. Soon, the quiet peaceful stillness of the evening would be interrupted by shocks of violence and hatred and all the malice that humanity could muster.

Despite all the wonders produced throughout the life of Christ, the debt was still unpaid. It would require more than His life. It would require His death as well, a merciless brutal death. The note was due tomorrow. Jesus was the only man on earth who had the resources to redeem all the inhabitants of the earth.

Burdened by the horror only hours away, Jesus called His disciples together and said:

"Do not let your hearts be troubled. Trust in God; trust also in me. In the Father's house are many rooms; if it were not so, I would have told you. I am going there to prepare a place for you. And if I go and prepare a place for you, I will come back and take you to be with me that you also may be where I am. You know the way to the place where I am going."

Thomas said unto him, "Lord we don't know where you are going, so how can we know the way?"

Jesus answered, "I am the way and the truth and the life. No one comes to the Father except through me. If you really knew me, you would know my Father as well. From now on, you do know him and have seen him."

Philip said, "Lord, show us the Father and that will be enough for us." Jesus answered, "Don't you know me, Philip, even after I have been among you such a long time? Anyone who has seen me has seen the Father. How can you say, 'Show us the Father?' Don't you believe that I am in the Father, and the Father is in me?" (John 14: 1-10 NIV)

We see in this conversation the vast chasm between divinity and humanity. We sense in Jesus' words the agony that often accompanies patience, the sadness that comes from repeated disappointment, and the emptiness that comes with betrayal. We sense from the words of Thomas and Philip the dense cloud of doubt and the dull fleshy consciousness we all possess. At least they were honest. At least they were sincere. Honesty and sincerity are wonderful qualities, precursors to repentance, but will not get us into Heaven. We need something more. We need a savior.

Jesus determined that his disciples should have assimilated much more than they had over the last three and a half years. He was dismayed that their belief system was still so immature, far too immature to drink from His cup. There had been no shortage of information and experience in their training. These eleven men had been awarded the privilege of front row seats to the greatest show on earth, even endowed with divine power at various times to perform miracles themselves.

There was no defect in the plan, the presentation, or the presenter, yet they remained remarkably humanistic, which is to remain deaf and dumb to the reality of Eternity, until such a time as the miracle of spiritual transformation is complete.

Henry David Thoreau once said, "It's not what you look at that matters, it's what you see." The disciples saw Jesus as a liberator, someone on the scale of King David, someone who would restore Israel to its rightful place, someone who would revive the glory days of King Solomon. Despite the consistent and contrary teachings of Jesus, that His kingdom was not of this world, the disciples persisted with their self-absorbed, soft and sentimental delusion of an economic and political kingdom. Though only a step away from Eternal truth, they were unwilling to trade in their hopes for His. They could not see beyond the social gospel, or the prosperity gospel, despite the fact that Jesus constantly reminded them that this world is only a bleep on the radar of Eternity.

This was not the first conversation Jesus had with His disciples concerning the scope of His kingdom and the essence of who He was. We go backwards now to an earlier time, a more peaceful time, when Jesus prodded the minds of His disciples to help them see that He really was God in human flesh. It was the previous spring when Jesus began to carve time out of his busy schedule for some private time with His disciples.

Normally, in His public ministry, Jesus traveled south from His home base of Capernaum. He rarely traveled north as He did this time. This time, He led His disciples away from the usual needy crowds and the taunting Pharisees to the pagan city of Caesarea Philippi. There is no indication that He traveled there for any other reason except to be left alone with His disciples to perform an amazing transfiguration and affirm the substance of the following conversation:

When Jesus came to the region of Caesarea Philippi, he asked His disciples, "who do people say the Son of Man is?"

They replied, "Some say John the Baptist; others say Elijah; still others, Jeremiah or one of the prophets."

"But what about you?" he asked. "Who do you say I am?"

Simon Peter answered, "You are the Christ, the Son of the living God."

Jesus replied, "Blessed are you, Simon son of Jonah, for this was not revealed to you by man, but by my Father in heaven. And I tell you that you are Peter, and on this rock I will build my church, and the gates of Hades will not overcome it."(Matthew 16:13-18 NIV)

Jesus did not need to question His disciples or anyone else to find out anything. He was not lacking for information. He already knew the answers before He asked the questions. His questions were never for His benefit but for the benefit of His listeners.

The first question, "Who do people say I am" is a broad sweeping statement which invokes the disciples, and us, to consider the ignorant and biased and fickle nature of public opinion. Jesus knew that public opinion was highly speculative and changed like the wind. The disciples affirmed it in their answer-- some say this. . . some say that. . . very likely, some will say tomorrow the opposite of what they say today . . . who knows how the public goes . . . it's all relative to their perceived best interest. First, but not foremost, Jesus needed to make certain the disciples understood that public opinion could never be trusted.

But then, Jesus asked the foremost question, the crucial question, the most critical question He ever asked. And still today the most important question for every human being. Our eternal destiny depends on how we answer the next question. "Who do YOU say I am?" With this penetrating question, Jesus instantly moves His disciples, and us, from the distant to the present, from public to private, from general to specific, from speculative to substantive, from collective to individual. There comes a time when Jesus jerks every one of us out of our casual and caviler mind set, backs us into a corner, and gets face to face and highly personal. With His blazing eyes penetrating into the depths of our soul, with nowhere to run, He says to every one of us, individually—not your brother, not your sister, not your mama, not your daddy, not your teacher, not your preacher—but YOU! WHO DO YOU SAY I AM???

Jesus was never confused about His identity. He spoke clearly and unapologetically about who he was and what he came to do. Here, I use some of Jesus' own words from the gospel of John to summarize who He claimed to be:

John 4:26 . . . I that speak to you are He (Messiah).

5:30 . . . I seek not my own will but the will of the Father that sent me.

6:35 . . . I am the bread of life he that cometh to me shall never hunger.

8:23 . . . Ye are from beneath I am from above.

8:58 . . . Before Abraham was I.

9:37 . . . It is He (Messiah) that talketh to thee.

10:30 . . . I and my Father are one.

12:44 . . . He that believeth one me believeth on Him who sent me.

13:13 . . . Ye call me Master and Lord and ye say

well for so I am.

13:31 . . . Now is the Son of man glorified and God is glorified in Him.

 14:6 . . . I am the way the truth and the life, no man cometh to the Father but by me.

14:11 . . . Believe me that I am in the Father and the Father in me.

16:28 . . . I came forth from the Father and am come into the world.

 17:5 . . . And now O Father glorify thou me with thine own self with the glory which I had with Thee before the world was.

Occasionally, someone who considers himself fairly intelligent will say something stupid, something like, "Jesus never really claimed to be the Son of God." O really? Where in the Bible does it say that? We know then that these amateur philosophers have never read the Bible, or they have a good case of willful ignorance, the very kind of pride that slams the doors of Heaven shut tighter than a Pharisee's purse. It is likely that such a person inspired C.S. Lewis (1898-1963) to respond with one of the most profound and most quoted perspectives of who Jesus really was. From his classic book, Mere Christianity, here is what Lewis had to say:

"I am trying here to prevent anyone saying the really foolish thing that people often say about Him (Jesus): 'I am ready to accept Jesus as a great moral teacher, but I don't accept His claim to be God.' That is the one thing we must not say. A man who was merely a man and said the sort of things that Jesus said would not be a great moral teacher. He would be either a lunatic—on a level with the man who says he is a poached egg—

or else he would be the Devil of Hell. You must make your choice. Either this man was, and is, the Son of God: or else a madman or something worse. You can shut Him up for a fool, you can spit at Him and kill Him as a demon; or you can fall at His feet and call Him Lord and God. But let us not come with any patronizing nonsense about His being a great human teacher. He has not left that open to us. He did not intend to."

Lewis reminds us that there are not that many options concerning the identity of Jesus. If we are honest and open minded to the gospel, we can rule out two of the three. The following is one of many common sense narratives concerning the identity of Jesus. It was proposed by a well respected religious leader who was somewhat familiar with Jesus. He, like many people today, had difficulty accepting Jesus for who He was, but he was willing to give Jesus an honest hearing. The conversation takes place after Jesus' death and resurrection, when the disciples had been arrested by the religious leaders for preaching the gospel. The hearing is recorded by Dr. Luke in the book of Acts 5:34-39 NIV:

But a Pharisee named Gamaliel, a teacher of the law, who was honored by all the people, stood up in the Sanhedrin and ordered that the men be put outside for a little while. Then he addressed them: "Men of Israel, consider carefully what you intend to do to these men. Some time ago Theudas appeared, claiming to be somebody, and about four hundred men rallied to him. He was killed, all his followers were dispersed, and it all came to nothing. After him, Judas the Galilean appeared in the days of the census and led a band of people in revolt. He too was killed, and all his followers scattered. Therefore, in the present case I advise you: Leave these men alone! Let them go! For if their purpose or activity is of human origin, it will fail. But if it is from God, you will not be able to stop these men; you will only find yourselves fighting against God."

According to the logic of Gamaleil, the most respected intellect among his peers, that which is true has a way of winning out in due time. Gamaleil was not the first or last person to recognize that time is not a friend to a liar. Time has its way of exposing a lie. There is an old proverb, "give a man enough rope and he will hang himself." Gamaleil also knew enough about God to know it is not wise to square off against Him, He could easily outlasts His enemies, or, if He so desired, destroy them.

If Jesus was not who He said He was, certainly in due time, His name would be forgotten without any effort on the part of the Pharisees. Moreover, if Jesus was not who He said He was, the ensuing 2,000 years since that conversation should have erased His memory from the face of the earth, and His influence on today's world should be far less significant than that of Edsel Ford.

But, that is far from reality. Unlike Theudas, Judas, and thousands of other reformers, rebels, and rulers, whose names have fallen into the great abyss of obscurity, Jesus' name remains constantly in the hearts and on the lips of millions. Jesus' name still saturates society, shouted from housetops and pulpits, whispered in reverent prayers in the still quietness of solitude by grateful millions who have been released from their chains of selfishness, hopelessness, and meaninglessness.

In history, we find countless attempts to extinguish His name and His teachings; Bibles have been banned and burned; His followers have been, and still are persecuted, many martyred for their unwillingness to deny Him; His name has been, and still is, distorted and slandered by secular elite; the humanist movement shrugs at His commandments and fights desperately to replace them with their utopian visions of earthly grandeur; relativist thinkers declare his ideas obsolete and seek to destroy any thought of absolutes and reorganize the world under a constitution of ever changing amendments.

Despite all, Jesus marches on with His faithful and fierce remnant who is undeterred by the resistance they face. His true followers not only know His Word, they know His Voice. They know that those who hate Jesus will hate them too. They know also that the gates of hell are of no consequence to them. Their face is set like flint, they have put their hand to the plow; and for them, there is no looking back.

In his book, "Who is Jesus," Tim Lahaye revealed some interesting thoughts expressed by Napoleon Bonaparte concerning the identity of Jesus:

"From first to last, Jesus is the same: always the same— majestic and simple, infinitely severe and infinitely gentle. Throughout a life passed under the public eye, He never gives occasion to find fault. The prudence of His conduct compels our admiration by its union of force and gentleness. Alike in speech and action, He is enlightened, consistent, and calm. Sublimity is said to be an attribute of divinity: what name, then, shall we give Him in whose character were united every element of the sublime?

I know men; and I tell you that Jesus is not a man. Everything in Him amazes me. His spirit outreaches mine, and His will confounds me. Comparison is impossible between Him and any other being in the world. He is truly a being by Himself. His ideas and His sentiments; the truth that He announces; His manner of convincing; are all beyond humanity and the natural order of things.

His birth, the story of His life; the profoundness of His doctrine, which overturns all difficulties, and is their most complete solution; His Gospel; the singularity of His mysterious being; His appearance; His empire; His progress through all centuries and kingdoms; all this is to me a prodigy; an unfathomable mystery.

I see nothing here of man. Near as I may approach, closely as I may examine, all remains above my comprehension—great with a greatness that crushes me. It is in vain that I reflect—all remains unaccountable!

I defy you to cite another life like that of Christ."

In his most recent book, "The Reason For My Hope," Billy Graham extends the thoughts of Napoleon by quoting writer John Abbot's research on Napoleon's characterization of Jesus:

". . .Superficial minds see a resemblance between Christ and the founders of empires and the gods of other religions. That resemblance does not exist. . . I search in vain in history to find the similar to Jesus Christ, or any thing which can approach the gospel. Neither history, nor humanity, nor the ages, nor nature offer me any thing with which I am able to compare it or to explain it. Here every thing is extraordinary. The more I consider the gospel, the more I am assured that there is nothing there which is not beyond the march of events and above the human mind . . .You speak of Caesar, of Alexander; of their conquests, and of the enthusiasm which they enkindled in the hearts of their soldiers. But can you conceive of a dead man making conquests, with an army faithful and entirely devoted to his memory. My armies have forgotten me, even while living, as the Carthaginian army forgot Hannibal. Such is our power! . . . Alexander, Caesar, Charlemagne, and myself founded empires. But upon what did we rest the creations of our genius? Upon force. Jesus Christ alone founded his empire upon love; and at this hour millions of men would die for him."

Napoleon was considered by many historians as one of the greatest political and military visionaries in history. He was broad minded and purposeful. He was alert and attentive to realities and forces that rule the universe, realities and forces he tried to harness to achieve his lofty goals. There have always been brilliant minds similar to his, but they lose their brilliance when they deny the deity of Jesus. They become narrow and biased and bound up in a circular rut, a rut that eventually becomes their grave.

Billy Graham, again from his most recent book, quotes theologian and historian Philip Schaff:

"This Jesus of Nazareth, without money and arms, conquered more millions than Alexander, Caesar, Mohammed, and Napoleon; without science and learning, he shed more light on things human and divine than all philosophers and scholars combined; without the eloquence of schools, he spoke such words of life as were never spoken before or since, and produced effects which lie beyond the reach of any orator or poet; without writing a single line, he set more pens in motion, and furnished themes for more sermons, orations, discussions, learned volumes, works of art, and sweet songs of praise, than the whole army of great men of ancient and modern times."

Sometimes it is the obvious that escapes us, and the familiar that we take for granted. I conclude this chapter with three anonymous writers who emphasize the obvious and the familiar to help us crystallize the powerful influence that Jesus has had, and continues to have, on the world as we know it:

Jesus the Teacher

He never taught a lesson in a classroom. . . He had no tools to work with, no blackboards, maps or charts. . . He used no subject outlines, kept no records, gave no grades, and His only text was ancient and well-worn. . . His students were the poor, the lame, the deaf, the blind, the outcast-and His method was the same for all who came to hear and learn. . . He opened eyes with faith. . . He opened ears with simple truth, and opened hearts with love, a love born of forgiveness. . . a gentle man, a humble man, He asked and won no honors, no gold awards of tribute to His expertise or wisdom. . . and yet this quiet Teacher from the hills of Galilee has fed the needs, fulfilled the hopes and changed the lives of many millions. . . for what He taught brought Heaven to earth and God's heart to all.

One Solitary Life

He was born in an obscure village, the child of a peasant woman. He grew up in another obscure village. He worked in a carpenter shop until He was thirty. He never wrote a book. He never held an office. He didn't go to college. He never visited a big city. He never traveled more than two hundred miles from the place He was born. He did none of the things usually associated with greatness. He had no credentials but Himself. He was only thirty-three when public opinion turned against Him, His friends ran away. One of them denied Him. He was turned over to His enemies and went through a mockery of a trial. He was nailed to a cross between two thieves. While He was dying, His executioners gambled for His clothing, the only property He had on earth. He was laid in a borrowed grave. Nineteen centuries have come and gone, and today He is the central figure of the human race and the leader of mankind's progress. All the armies that ever marched, all the navies that ever sailed, all the parliaments that ever sat, all the kings that ever reigned, have not affected the life of man on this earth as much as . . . this one solitary life.

The Incomparable Christ

More than nineteen centuries ago there was a man born contrary to the laws of life. This man lived in poverty and was reared in obscurity. He did not travel extensively. Only once did He cross the boundary of the country in which He lived; that was during His exile in childhood. He possessed neither wealth nor influence. His relatives were inconspicuous, and had neither training nor formal education. In infancy He startled a king; in childhood He puzzled doctors; in manhood He ruled the course of nature, walked upon the billows as if pavements, and hushed the sea to sleep. He healed the multitudes without medicine and made no charge for His service. He never wrote a book, and yet the libraries of the country could not hold the books that have been written about Him. He never wrote a song, and yet He has furnished the theme for more songs than all the songwriters combined. He never founded a college, but all the schools put together cannot boast of having as many students. He never marshaled an army; nor drafted a soldier, fired a gun; and yet no leader ever had more volunteers who have, under His orders, made more rebels stack arms and surrender without a shot fired. He never practiced psychiatry, and yet He has healed more broken hearts than all the doctors far and near. Once each week the wheels of commerce cease their turning and multitudes wend their way to worshiping assemblies to pay homage and respect to Him. The names of the past proud statesmen of Greece and Rome have come and gone. The names of the past scientists, philosophers, and theologians have come and gone; but the name of this man abounds more and more. Though time has spread nineteen hundred years between the people of this generation and the scene of the crucifixion, He still lives. Herod could not destroy Him, and the grave could not hold Him. He stands forth upon the highest pinnacle of heavenly glory, proclaimed of God, acknowledged by angels, adored by saints, and feared by devils, as the living, personal Christ, our Lord and Savior. We are either going to be forever with Him, or forever without Him. It was the incomparable Christ who said: "Behold, I stand at the door, and knock: If any man hear my voice, and open the door, I will come in to him, and will sup with him, and he with me. . ." (Revelation 3:20) "I am the way, the truth, and the life: no man cometh unto the Father, but by me." (John 14:6)

What is your response to Jesus' question: WHO DO YOU SAY I AM???

"I must be about my Father's business"

LUKE 2:49

"I must be about my Father's business"

L U K E   2 : 4 9

Chapter 2

Thirty A. D. was a time in history remarkably different from our modern world, yet the hearts and souls of men were strikingly identical to our own. There is very little evolution in how people come to believe what they believe. We believe and disbelieve today upon the same basis we always have, despite vast stretches of time and space and a kaleidoscope of variables. Human nature is bound together from beginning to end with an indestructible ancestral cord. Ten thousand years does not transform a man. Only God can. The process is the same today as it was in Jesus' day, each individual must grant God permission to take up residence within.

In a democratic world, we believe what we want to believe, the way we graze a Sunday buffet. We have been awarded that right. Unfortunately, we often believe wrongly and incompletely, wearing our wills on our sleeves, so much so that we will squint our eyes and grit our teeth and deny the glaring facts that prove us wrong. Yes, "the light came into the world, but men ran from the light, preferring the darkness which better hides their wicked deeds." In that respect, nothing has changed. Pride is still the patriarch of all our sins.

Against the dark drab backdrop of desperate secular history, the bottom hatch of heaven swung open and the Divine Light descended. Down He came, pulsating through the darkness, gravitating humbly to the lowest spot, like bottom feeders sink to the ocean floor. It is a long and treacherous journey from earth to Heaven, but it is not far from Heaven to earth.

At the earthly entrance of the infinite gulf stands that narrow gate, but from Heaven's perspective the funnel is reversed. The pearly gates swing wide. The deck seems to be stacked against the lost, the narrow gate difficult to find; but light travels true and fast, and even the smallest ray of Divine Light is easy for the repentant sinner to follow.

The one and only God sent His one and only Son down to earth, not by chance, not on a whim, but by design. He arrived on time for Christmas, but it would be another thirty Christmases before He would reveal His purpose to the public. The infant Son of God blended naturally and seamlessly into the landscape of humanity, just another cog in the wheel of a very common family.

He had to use His five senses like you and I. He took up residence as the son of an obscure carpenter, learning to build earthly things with His heavenly hands, learning to be a producer, not merely a consumer. Later, he habitually advertised His Divine ideal for humanity—"seek to serve, not to be served."

As a young man Jesus appeared normal. His exceptionality was temporarily suspended though fully existing in His infinite past and future. He had to learn his abc's and the multiplication table. Like you and I, He learned to taste His own sweat. He learned the sting of an inerrant hammer's blow, the ache of weariness and the pang of hunger; He learned to love the soft and soothing voice of His mother as she called for quiet and reverent family meals; He became tickled by the ploys and pranks that tumbled incessantly out of His brothers and sisters; He loved to hear the same six words you and I love to hear, "well done good and faithful servant."

He loved His simple life, relishing even the menial and repetitious, unlike most of humanity. Only the deeply spiritual man can squeeze a blessing out of the mundane, or find peace in longsuffering. For those in and around the tiny village of Nazareth, His childhood seemed so happily common and insignificant. Over the years, even His family seemed to forget who He was. Time in the context of daily demands will play tricks on the mind, deceiving us, making us forget what should never be forgotten.

Eventually, His terse lifespan would barely stretch one third of what we now call the first century A.D. And the essence of His mission on earth would be completed in just three short years, hardly enough time to accomplish anything of lasting value. But, He only needed a short time. Eternal work is not confined or defined by time, but by God.

Jesus had visited earth briefly many times before He arrived in person. Before He came in the flesh, He came clothed as "The Angel of the Lord." Previously, He picked his spots as He intervened providentially. But this glorious time, reality enveloped theophany and fulfilled prophecy. The Word became flesh. God inhabited a human body. This new and long awaited miracle was universally unprecedented, nothing ever like it, before or since. It is a mystery no one has ever or will ever comprehend.

Amazingly, He chose not to arrive in maturity. He chose instead to come as a mere embryo, hanging the essence of life upon the crux of conception, giving life in the womb His blessing. He christened the lonely life of gestation as a marvelous sign of Divinity. Today, millions of brand new souls, created no less in the image of God than our own soul, camp out in the womb and wait patiently and innocently and hopefully, as Christ Himself once waited, for their appointed time and purpose. Yet those with their gift of life in full bloom fight pridefully and selfishly to deny life to those less mature. It's a woman's right they drone to dispense justice on the hopeful soul bound and gagged inside her womb. Who assigned a woman the right to destroy the life inside her? God did not! His patience again is wearing thin.

Yes, God eased into earth quietly in the fullness of time, on His own terms; no thunder, no lightning, no fanfare. His arrival was not the front page news of the day. He slipped in humbly, undetected by the mass of humanity, except for some local shepherds and an obscure band of foreign wise men, spell bound by an ancient prophecy and the strange and persistent Star that confirmed it.

Of course, the angels had saved the date; they had it marked on their celestial calendars for centuries and would not have missed it for the world. They filled the skies and celebrated wildly, but few here on earth seemed to notice save the lowly shepherds and the attentive wise men. Wise men have always been the most neglected minority, just as the modern world ignores His second coming, the ancients ignored His first.

The world was not ready for Him, nor worthy of Him. There was no place prepared, no spacious room, no warm bed, no soft pillow; nothing, except his mother's breast and the strong and rugged arms of a carpenter. There in that desolate and empty place, the family unit alone proved sufficient to embrace and protect God's only Son. It is obvious today that God ordained the family unit as the foundation of society, consequently, the world prospers in the same degree that the family unit prospers.

The sanctity of one man and one woman in holy matrimony rose up and proved His Grace sufficient. Baby Jesus found His needs met by nature, through motherhood, and fatherhood, just as His Father designed it. Baby Jesus found what every child should find in family---nourishment, warmth, rest, safety, peace, laughter, joy, hope, truth; but more importantly, the kind of love that never fails.

Jesus voluntarily forfeited his heavenly privileges when He arrived on earth, consequently time and space grabbed hold of Him and treated Him not like the God he was, but like the rest of us. His omniscience was suspended and dispensed on a need to know basis, His omnipresence gave way to His early morning prayers, and His omnipotence was controlled and directed from above.

Heaven and earth are very different places. Heaven is the pure and perfect Eternal playground, earth a temporary and greatly flawed battleground. Down here, we have to fight to survive. We have three powerful enemies—the world, the flesh, and the devil. Evil always lurks in the shadows, seeking to destroy that which is good and right. Satan, the prince of this world, the roaring lion, sought to slay the baby Jesus from the beginning, but the Father protected the Son, as fathers should.

Time passed and Mary birthed additional children. Eventually, Jesus had four little brothers and at least two younger sisters. Mary frequently pondered the mysteries of her past. Mary's memories were like our own, more a part of us than our arms and legs. She often pondered over her eldest son's heavenly origin, His supernatural conception, the visits from angels and wise men, the dreams, the fulfillment of ancient prophecy; and she often wondered why she was selected as the mother of the

Son of God. It was all too large to forget or to understand. But the events themselves, the ones that provoked her thoughts, had now slipped deeper and deeper into history, and history has a way of fading and shading and depreciating the original value of events and experiences. The present and the practical are not particularly nostalgic.

After twelve years, the duties of motherhood demanded more and more of her focus, forcing her memories toward dormancy. This might help explain how one day she lost the Son of God. It was on a routine trip to Jerusalem for the Passover and the subsequent trip home when she realized that her eldest son was missing. The caravan had traveled north a full day when Jesus did not show up for the evening meal. She and Joseph searched the caravan with no success. It soon became evident that Jesus was not with any of the friends with which he customarily traveled.

Had He been kidnapped to be sold into slavery as was Joseph of old? Traveling was very dangerous in those days and places, and safety was in numbers. Jesus was now alone or so they imagined. Had He been attacked by wild animals or robbers and left to die in some unknown desolate place? Was He trying to catch up to the caravan? Had He gotten lost along the way? Was He out there somewhere dying of hunger and thirst and exposure? Had He spoke openly and honestly and prematurely about His true identity to the wrong people and been arrested for blasphemy? These and thoughts like these occupied the mind of Mary and Joseph as they hurriedly and frantically back tracked their way to the city, putting themselves in harm's way.

Three days of terror transported them through the crowded streets of Jerusalem and into the courts of the temple. To their amazement, there in the midst of the most learned men of the day sat little twelve year old Jesus. He was sitting there safely and contently, as undisturbed as a man would sit fishing on a river bank. He was happily answering the questions of men who supposedly had all the answers. These elite Bible scholars were obviously mesmerized by His wisdom.

But Mary and Joseph were not mesmerized. Instead, they were distressed by His apparent lack of responsibility and blatant unconcern for His personal safety and that of His parents. How could He be so careless as to put His parents through the terror of the last three days? Was He not mature enough to realize the extent of His foolishness?

Unable to restrain her patience any longer, Mary chastised her Son saying, "Son, why have you treated us like this? Your father and I have been anxiously searching for you." (Luke 2:48 NIV) Mary's question was perfectly natural and reasonable. As parents, we have all been there, we have all asked the "why" question to our children… "why did you do that… what in the world were you thinking."   And as children, we have all been asked the "why" question on a number of occasions. Rarely, do we come up with the appropriate answer. Most often, when we do the unexpected, we never stop to consider why.

The "why" questions are often the most difficult to answer. It is because the "why" questions have the inherent intent to discover a good reason, a motive, and ultimately a purpose for everything we say and do, and in a broader context, for everything that happens. The problem is that the origin of an ultimate purpose goes back beyond our existence. We are incapable of finding the answer within ourselves. We must delve into Eternity to find our answers.

All "why" questions are encoded with the assumption that there is an answer, and all "why" questions are irrelevant if there is no answer. Why did the chicken cross the road? Obviously, there is a reason the chicken crossed the road even though the chicken may not waste a lifetime meditating upon it like men invariably do. And there is likewise a reason for everything we say and do. Cause and effect is not only foundational in human logic, it is foundational in Creation. There is a reason! There is a plan! There is a design! It is not always obvious to us what the reason or the plan or the design is; and even when it is obvious, it is more our desire to deny it, or conceal it, or obstruct it, rather than embrace it, or obey it, or confess it.

Jesus was plugged in to Eternity. There were no gaps or lapses in transmission and reception. He never had any difficulty coming up with the appropriate answer. He was constantly in tune with the Eternal flow of answers. He was also the most transparent person who ever walked the face of the earth, always willing to reveal the answer. He had no sin to distort His responses, as we humans do. Even as a twelve year old, He had nothing to hide. He responded to His distressed parents directly and honestly, and, from a purely human perspective, surprisingly, "Why were you searching for me? Didn't you know I had to be in my Father's house?"

In modern day language, culture, and standards in parent-child relationships there seems to be some irresponsibility and even some disrespect in Jesus' answer. Certainly His answer is not the one we expected. We anticipated a more humble and apologetic reply, a softer and warmer response. Perhaps a better understanding of the ancient language, culture, and the particular relationship Jesus had with His parents would dismiss any notion of irreverence or irresponsibility as some have suggested. But there is a much greater revelation in Jesus' answer.

To Mary and Joseph, His character was never in question. They knew well His sinlessness. However, there was such an overwhelming openness and innocence and truthfulness in His answer that it jolted His mother, abruptly putting her relationship with her Son back into context, sending her all the way back through history to her virginity, when an angel from God appeared with an unusual birth announcement. Sometimes the words of our children snatch us back into reality. Jesus' words always have a way of reviving deep and dormant memories and transforming them into reality. He always puts things in the context of the Eternal.

His response restored His mother's spiritual perspective, which is what Jesus always did in all His conversations. He never allowed His mind to center upon the material, as men invariably do. He always reached downward and invited people upward, never compromising His deity, never lowering or compromising His spiritual standard, never losing sight of His mission and never apologizing for the self-denial He required from His followers.

Mary's mind raced back to His infant dedication ceremony in very temple where she now stood twelve years earlier. Mary, mother of Jesus, rapidly replayed the precious memory she had saved securely from when Jesus was only eight days old. She recalled the glow in the face of Simeon, the old priest who had prayed to God to keep him alive just long enough to see the promised Messiah.

At the sight of the infant Jesus, the old priest beamed with joy, took Him up in his arms and blessed God and said, "Lord, now letteth thou thy servant depart in peace, according to thy word: for mine eyes have seen thy salvation, which thou hast prepared before the face of all people; a light to lighten the Gentiles, and the glory of thy people Israel...behold, this child is set for the fall and rising again of many in Israel; and a sign which shall be spoken against."(Luke 2:29-32 KJV)

Mary, astonished then as now, remembered how at this point in his prophesy Simeon fastened his gaze upon her specifically, and mysteriously extended his prophesy, " a sword shall pierce through thy own soul also, that the thoughts of many hearts may be revealed."

What was Mary and Joseph to think of this new development? Was this the initial prick of the sword of which Simeon spoke? They knew the day was coming when Jesus would leave them to fulfill His destiny, but they had not anticipated it would come this soon. He was just a boy. We know from scripture that Jesus did not begin His ministry at this point. Instead, He returned to Nazareth with Mary and Joseph and managed to remain surprisingly scripturally silent for nearly two more decades.

What are you and I to think of this abrupt injection into the gospel narrative? What are we to take away from this very brief and puzzling conversation Jesus had with His parents, the first and only recorded conversation during the first thirty years of Jesus' life? What does it mean? Why was it recorded?

I believe this short conversation contains the very essence of Jesus' life on earth, and it reveals His awareness of it at an early age. With the first recorded words to come from His lips, Jesus identified Himself as the Son of God. As a twelve year old, He proclaimed His deity. And, He did something else of critical importance. He explicitly identified His mission, and implicitly ours. He answered the "why" question for us all, once and for all. He was on earth solely to serve the Father! And so are we.

"Wist ye not that I must be about my Father's business?" (Luke 2:49KJV) Obviously, He was not speaking of His earthly father, Joseph, or He would have never left the caravan. This was the first of many clear affirmations from the mouth of Jesus concerning His identity and His purpose.

What was His Father's business? Throughout the gospels Jesus identified numerous reasons for His earthly visit. Here in short summary from John's gospel in His own words are some of the specifics:

> **John 3:13** …I came not to condemn, but to save.
> **John 5:43** …to represent the Father.
> **John 6:26** …to give Eternal life.
> **John 6:38** …to do the will of the Father.
> **John 9:39** …to give sight to the blind.
> **John 10:10** …to bring life more abundant.
> **John 12:27** …to bring glory to the Father.
> **John 12:46** …as a light to a dark world.
> **John 14:49** …to reveal what the Father is like.

The reader should read John's gospel in context to experience greater meaning of what Jesus was saying. And there are many other such affirmations, throughout the gospels, making it impossible to misinterpret who He was and why He was here on earth.

What does all of this mean to you and me? If Jesus was who He said He was, then my identity and purpose must come from Him. My destiny depends on him, my origin linked back to Him. Personal happiness is preceded by personal holiness. In the words of Rick Warren, "we were made for His pleasure." We cannot find a permanent sense of peace and joy anywhere else. We cannot find a lasting fulfillment in anyone else. The ultimate essence of life for all humanity is bound up in Jesus, the Son of God. He is the WHY. He is the reason we exist.

"Man shall not live by bread alone"

MATTHEW 4 : 4

"Man shall not live by bread alone"

MATTHEW 4:4

Chapter 3

Over half a century has not erased the memory of my elementary school teachers. Some I remember more vividly, for some made a greater impression than others. But I still remember them all. I remember well the day Ms. Rogers, my second grade teacher, handed out a little pamphlet. We had started the school year in the old school, in the room nearest the boy's bathroom; but now, we had moved two miles west, to the new school, on the east wing, in the second room from the playground. I remember the smell of fresh concrete, and the temptation to write "Terry was here" on the pristine bathroom wall. I remember the ceiling looked like it was made of straw and wet toilet paper stuck well to it.

I was still meditating on the sufficiency of the straw ceiling, and wiping the dampness off my hands when Ms. Rogers handed me my little pamphlet. She instructed us to carefully observe all the pictures therein, and to draw an X through the objects that looked out of place. She gave us some examples: "Look at the first picture," she said, "there is a horse, a cow, a goat, and a bale of hay…which one does not belong with the others?" "The hay," we surmised. "You are right" she said, "now put a big X through the hay because the hay is not an animal and does not belong."

"Now, look at the second picture;" continued Ms. Rogers, "there is a shovel, a rake, a hoe, and a duck…which one does not belong?" The class responded in unison, "the duck!" We quickly X'd the duck and proceeded to post the appropriate X's throughout the pamphlet. As a second grader, l thought school was incredibly simple and took up too much of the time between recesses. All of life seemed so incredibly simple back then.

I did not know at the time that I was taking a test. I did not know that my performance on Ms. Roger's tests would determine whether I would repeat the second grade, or move on to the third. I did not know that as I grew older the tests would become more complex and more difficult; that I would be judged a success or failure by my test scores.

I did not know there would be many more important tests awaiting me, most of them outside the walls of a school. I did not have a clue at the time that soon the very foundations on which the tests were based would begin to crumble; that the boundary lines so clear in those days would be expanded to give Dick and Jane more room to experiment with strange new identities.

I did not know that the intended consequences would eventually produce a brand new world, a world hell bent and determined to throw out the old stable traditional values. If I had known, being the curious sort that I am, I probably would have asked, "WHY???... why would somebody want to destroy our treasured traditional values? What kind of person would do such a thing?"

But, I did not know enough to ask. Nor did I know of the tragic results yet to come from this new liberating agenda, a utopianism packaged and sold under the banner of "progress." How could a second grader have known that these new "progressive" ideas would spin us into a confused and chaotic planet with no resemblance to the simple definitive world I knew as a child? I was clueless. I trusted adults to do the right thing. I did not know enough to even consider that there was an evil purpose for it all; that someone had conceived it, designed it, and was behind it calling the shots.

It is fair enough to say I was ignorant of what was going on in the world around me, and even moreso, within me. I have since learned a little. I have since learned that the sin is not in being ignorant, but in staying ignorant. The sin lies in the apathy that ignores the truth and perpetuates the ignorance. I have learned that the worst and most prominent kind of ignorance is this apathetic willful ignorance, the kind of ignorance that elevates personal pleasure or personal gain above right and wrong, the kind of stubborn ignorance that entices us to tolerate a wrong so long as it supplies a specific benefit to some special group of people.

It is not that most people cannot discern the truth. The essence of the problem is that most people prefer the lie. If the general public were to acknowledge a few simple self-evident truths, they would have to change. They would be forced to change their perspective, consequently, their world-view, and eventually their lifestyle. Jesus nailed the willful ignorant to the wall when he said, "...the light came into the world, but people preferred the darkness because it better hid their evil deeds..."(John 3:19-20) The old prophet Jeremiah nailed us all to the wall when he said, "...the heart of man is desperately wicked, who can know it..."(Jeremiah 17:9)

If we study the conversations of Jesus we can trace this "so-called" new agenda back to its origin. We can begin to recognize the deceit and understand who is responsible for it, how we are deceived by it, and more importantly, how to defeat it. As a bonus, we can also learn something about test taking. Consider this two thousand year old conversation Jesus had with the devil. It is recorded in Matthew 4:1-11: (also in Mark 1: 12, 13; Luke 4: 1-13)

Then Jesus was led by the Spirit into the desert to be tempted by the devil. After fasting forty days and forty nights, He was hungry. The tempter came to Him and said, "If you are the Son of God, tell these stones to become bread." Jesus answered, "It is written: "Man does not live by bread alone, but on every word that comes from the mouth of God." Then the devil took Him to the "holy city" and had Him stand on the highest point of the temple. "If you are the Son of God," he said, "throw yourself down. For it is written: "He will command His angels concerning you, and they will lift you up in their hands, so that you will not strike your foot against a stone." Jesus answered him, "It is also written: Do not put the Lord your God to the test." Again, the devil took Him to a very high mountain and showed Him all the kingdoms of the world and their splendor. "All of this I will give you," he said, "if you will bow down and worship me." Jesus said to Him, "Away from me Satan! For it is written: Worship the Lord your God, and serve Him only." Then the devil left Him, and the angels came and attended Him.

The spiritual subtleties of this conversation are too numerous and too vast to discuss in a few pages, but a few significant points are obvious. First, there is the brevity of the narrative, from which we may surmise is the preferred standard when conversing with the devil. Second, there is Jesus' simple and consistent reliance upon God's Written Word to defeat the assaults of the most powerful representative of evil, thus illustrating the supremacy and sufficiency of the Bible. Third, there is the seemingly radical assessment that even a starving man has a greater need than food. This doctrine supports one of the most dominate teachings of Jesus—the revelation that human beings are not merely material creatures, but spiritual beings, designed and destined to live beyond this world and throughout Eternity. And fourth, Jesus stuck with the original plan, rejecting the devil's new agenda–the liberating agenda which proposes that man can live by bread alone. Jesus assures and reassures us that the original plan is superior to any "ism" the devil can invent, whether it be humanism or materialism or relativism or whatever "ism" mankind can dream up.

From a literary perspective, the narrative is surprisingly simple. It produces two main characters—Jesus, and the devil. The plot is based upon the common and familiar age old conflict between good and evil. The setting has only three stops, moving quickly and easily from the floor of an unnamed desert to the highest point of the temple, and finally, higher yet, to the highest peak in the region. This geography was very familiar to Jesus and the devil and consistent with what inhabitants and visitors of the holy land experience today.

The mood of the narrative is somber and serious; starvation has a way of snubbing triviality, frivolity, hilarity, and ultimately, hope. The devil knows well that starvation also has a way of producing desperation, which opens up the mind to options that exist outside the will of God. Such grave circumstances excite the opportunistic nature of the devil who always exploits every advantage.

This should be regarded as a matter of severe importance
to us all in times of testing, thus the old proverb, "the devil is
always in the details." It is not a coincidence that our most
difficult tests seem to come when we have descended to our
weakest and most vulnerable points.

From the very start of the narrative, the deck is stacked
against Jesus, and the odds are that Jesus will fall for the tricks of
the devil just as Adam did. But, Jesus does not buy what the
devil is selling. Why not? Jesus is a man like Adam. But He is
not all together identical to Adam. He is not just a man. He is at
once the perfect man and the perfect God, one hundred per cent
in both cases. He is an unfathomable, one-of-kind anomaly.
There is no imperfection in either nature. He had a job to do and
would not divert from it for the devil or anybody else. Embedded
in His words and actions was His destiny, a destiny sprawled out
before Him like an interstate highway, the same stubborn
preordained purpose which runs threadlike from Genesis through
Revelation.

A person reading the Bible for the first time may be
surprised or even shocked to find the persistent coexistence of
the here and now and the hereafter. In every instance and in
every circumstance they reside together, humanity and deity
paradoxically singular in the personhood of Jesus Christ. The
rookie Bible reader may also be confused or even dismayed to
find this coexistence of the material and the spiritual treated as a
normalcy in human beings, though certainly not as an equality.

Perhaps the inequality is best explained in scriptural
language–the material is "swallowed up" by the spiritual, or if
you prefer, the natural is "swallowed up" by the supernatural.
Again, from a literary perspective, the Bible does not go into
great detail to explain the superiority of the spirit over the flesh.
It is simply and repetitively stated as fact. There is a reason we

have no explanation. There are some things that God cannot dumb down enough for us to comprehend.

The substance of the Bible is spiritually discerned, going beyond the reach of language, and even action. It is our flesh that gets in the way. The minimum requirement for understanding the Bible is at least an open and honest mind concerning what we call the supernatural. An honest acknowledgement that there is a God is the necessary prerequisite to understanding what God is saying. As tragic as it is, it is reasonable to expect that the person who rejects the spiritual nature of man or the existence of God is locked out of understanding the Bible.

It is the nature of sovereignties to assume that we accept their ways as being higher than our ways. Among human beings it would be arrogance, but with God it is omniscience. The clay has no right to ask the potter anything. The Bible often asks us to accept without question what we cannot fully understand and what we may initially consider radical, or even harsh. The fundamental doctrine that humanity is temporarily physical and permanently spiritual is a prime example. The Bible has a scary word to describe the way we are to process such revelations. It is called faith.

There is no salvation by knowledge. It is by Grace through faith. And without faith no personal revelation is possible. Even with faith, we must learn to be content with a variety of mysteries. This faith issue, though not unreasonable, is very difficult for our modern day culture to accept. A culture born and bred to worship its own intellect and to pride itself in its ability explain everything is irritated by the pesky presence of the supernatural. Small petty prideful men quickly reject what they cannot explain, and a prideful culture always puts personal opinion and individual rights above everything else.

One of the most repetitive mistakes we Christians make is that we too often reverse the reality. It is a well published fact that we are subconsciously seduced by the material, even when we think we are doing otherwise. And, without a constant reminder, we are subject to completely ignore the spiritual. The material world is always in our face, dominating our senses, and we are lured into the trap of considering the material world the greater force, and sometimes, the only force.

Since the spiritual world is invisible, it is easy to see the effect and ignore the cause. It takes time and effort and experience to drive this revelation beyond our consciousness and deep into the subconscious. Maybe we are not at all times totally convinced that the body is temporary and the spirit eternal. I was intrigued with the way C.S. Lewis expressed this reality, and it often pops into my head when the subject of spirituality is being discussed… "you don't have a spirit," says Lewis, "you are a spirit, what you have is a body…" Write that paraphrase of scripture on your door post and hear the prophets sing, "Amen!"

I realize that I have rambled away from where I had planned to go in this essay. I have been realizing it for the last several paragraphs, but it seems I have had no great desire to quit rambling until now. As I have tried to express, the spirit, though it is often ignored, is far more powerful than the flesh, and when we allow the Holy Spirit to have His way, we sometimes end up where we had not planned to go. Now, I will attempt to return to where I was and finish this chapter with what I consider the major point of Jesus' conversation with the devil.

Jesus answered all three of the devil's attacks the same way. He quoted scripture. And in so doing, He demonstrated for us the great power in God's Written Word. He did not use any of His supernatural powers to defeat the devil. He simply used a supernatural book, a weapon which is readily available to us. We plainly see the Son of God powerfully endorsing the Word of God. It was His weapon of choice to defeat temptation, and it should be ours. It is obvious the lesson Jesus wants us to take away from His conversation with the devil is that we too should learn to rely on the unfailing authority of the Bible.

It should be noted that the devil knows scripture better than most Christians. He and his friends and a plentiful group of false prophets make a good living manipulating God's Word. This is a tactic we must expect from the devil and his demons and the useful idiots with impure motives. However clever the devil is, he cannot deceive the one who wrote it, or the ones who have a comprehensive knowledge of it. False prophets run like roaches when the light of the gospel is turned on.

Jesus quickly rebuked the devil for his attempt to manipulate scripture and continued to hammer him with the Old Testament book of Deuteronomy. Being exposed as the liar he was, and realizing he could not stand against God's written Word, the devil quickly retreated. Darkness is always chased away by light. When we have a fundamental understanding of the Bible, we too are able to shine the light and expose the deceit. False prophets cannot exist where God's Word is thoroughly understood.

I was surprised when I read of the popularity of the Bible, the world's bestselling book, having sold billions of copies, easily blowing away any competition.

But, I was disappointed when I read the various surveys concerning Bible reading. One recent survey stated that over 70% of Americans consider themselves Christians and believe the Bible to be the Word of God, but only 42% read the Bible occasionally, 34% once a week, and 12% daily. Even with a wide margin of error, it is clear why modern day Christianity fails to make the impact on society that it should. Bible illiteracy has reached an epidemic stage, making the church itself a playground for Satan. It is tragic that Christians do not know what it is they believe or why they believe it, but more tragically, they do not know the God in whom they believe, as He reveals Himself to us in His Word.

To begin to understand the Bible, I think it is important to examine what the Bible says about itself: its content, its uniqueness, its unity, its longevity, its accuracy, its authority, its authorship, its inerrancy, its sufficiency, its power, its effectiveness. Here are some of the scriptures scattered throughout the Bible which reference the Bible's claims concerning the preceding subjects:

John 1:1 In the beginning was the Word, and the Word was with God, and the Word was God.

2 Timothy 3:16 All Scripture is God-breathed and is useful for teaching, rebuking, correcting, and training in righteousness, so that the man of God may be thoroughly equipped for every good work.

Romans 15:4 For everything that was written in the past was written to teach us, so that through endurance and the encouragement of the scriptures we might have hope.

2 Peter 1:20-21 Above all, you must understand that no prophecy of Scripture came about by the prophet's own interpretation. For prophecy never had its origin in the will of man, but men spoke from God as they were carried along by the Holy Spirit.

1 Thessalonians 2:13 And we also thank God continually because, when you received the Word of God, which you heard from us, you accepted it not as the word of men, but as it actually is, the Word of God, which is at work in you who believe.

2 Peter 3:15 Bear in mind that our Lord's patience means salvation, just as our dear brother Paul also wrote you with the wisdom that God gave him.

Hebrews 1: 1-2 In the past God spoke to our forefathers through the prophets at many times and in various ways, but in these last days He has spoken to us by His Son, whom He appointed heir of all things.

Hebrews 4:12 For the Word of God is living and active. Sharper than any double-edged sword, it penetrates even to the dividing soul and spirit, joints and marrow; it judges the thoughts and attitudes of the heart.

Jeremiah 23:29 "Is not my Word like fire," declares the Lord, "and like a hammer that breaks a rock in pieces?"

John 6:63 The Spirit gives life; the flesh counts for nothing. The words I have spoken to you are Spirit and they are life.

Proverbs 4: 20-22 My son, pay attention to what I say; listen closely to my words. Do not let them out of your sight, keep them within your heart; for they are life to those who find them and health to a man's whole body.

Isaiah 55:11 …so is my Word that goes out from my mouth: It will not return to me empty, but will accomplish what I desire and achieve the purpose for which I sent it.

Isaiah 40:8 The grass withers and the flowers fade but the Word of our God stands forever.

Matthew 5:18 I tell you the truth, until heaven and earth disappear, not the smallest letter, nor the least stroke of the pen, will by any means disappear from the Law until everything is accomplished.

John 15: 7 If you remain in me and my words remain in you, ask whatever you wish, and it will be given you.

Proverbs 30:5-6 Every Word of God is flawless; he is a shield to those who take refuge in Him. Do not add to His words or He will rebuke you and prove you a liar.

Revelation 22:18-19 I warn everyone who hears the words of the prophecy of this book: If anyone adds anything to them, God will add to him the plagues described in this book. And if anyone takes words away from this book of prophecy, God will take away from him his share in the tree of life and in the holy city, which are described in this book.

Even the most rebellious and calloused skeptic must admit that the Bible is clear in its claims about itself. Over two thousand times the Bible uses such phrases as, "the Lord spoke unto Jonah, or the Word of the Lord came unto Jeremiah, or God said unto Moses, write these things down." It does not give us any wiggle room. It is not a book written by men. It has no respect for our opinion of it and never apologies for its dogmatism. It bids us to accept it or reject it but warns us consistently that we must never undermine it by distortion or misrepresentation.

God, with His first four words, reduced the ambitious theories of mankind to ambiguous equations. He crushed the babbling towers of human pride. With His words, "In the beginning God..." He snatched from the greedy hands of humanity its pampered elitism, its proud philosophies, its evolving sciences, its cultured aristocracy, its accumulated wealth and power, its novel and unique inventiveness.

His Creation thundered through the cosmos at the first sound of His voice, calibrating the speed of light, directing every atom to report promptly to its assigned place, canceling every other creative option, leaving every living soul dangling inescapably between denial and affirmation, dependent solely upon the same and solitary faculty–God's gift of free will.

As insurance, God mysteriously coded His explanation for our existence in the hungry heart of the humble masses, insuring that the ignorant and innocent child is equally as capable of assessing his origin, destiny and purpose as the aged and unrepentant scholar. He lovingly placed His own image within us that we may recognize His voice. This inherent favor, this "God-shaped vacuum," works in concert with our free will to levitate us toward Him, and to plead with us to return when we go the other way.

No human authored preamble encompasses the precedents which anchor the world to its frame. No other declaration can be more absolute. This is the way God presents Himself to us in His Word. This is the reality of God's Word.

A.W. Tozer defines reality this way: "Reality is that which has existence apart from any idea any mind may have of it, and which would exist if there were no mind anywhere to entertain a thought of it. That which is real has being in itself. It does not depend on the observer for its validity."

The Bible certainly reflects reality as it transverses the history of mankind, stopping at various intervals to reveal God's numerous attributes and to illuminate the particulars of the human condition. We soon see the obvious theme–the closer men come to God the better they fare, and the further from God they wander the more their troubles are multiplied.

Forty different authors over a period of fifteen hundred years agree on a singular message—that God has created man for Himself. How many philosophers agree on anything of significance on any given day? Take for example the three basic questions that philosophers are still debating: Where did man come from? Where is he going? Why is he here?

All forty authors are in full agreement that man was created by God, for God, and will live eternally with God or separated from Him in a place called hell. This simple and singular solution to mankind's most formidable dilemma is the golden thread that runs throughout God's Word. It is basic to understanding the Bible, so basic a second grader can understand it in one sitting, and at the same time, complex enough to keep a genius busy for a lifetime.

Invariably, just beneath the surface of every simple concept lies an amazingly complex network of variables. When we possess a thorough knowledge of God's Word we can conquer every challenge and pass every test by simply following the instructions of my second grade teacher, Ms. Rogers, who advised us-- "just look at the pictures and put a big "X" through the things that do not belong." If it is X'd in the Bible, it should be X'd from my life.

"No man can serve two masters"

MATTHEW 6:24

"No man can serve two masters"

MATTHEW 6:24

Chapter 4

Why should I waste my valuable time reading some dusty old book, littered with sketchy segments of history, freckled with absolute fantasy, written by a rag tag band of obscure and insecure old men who lived thousands of years ago; narrow minded men, biased at best; wedged into a paltry and blood drenched partial of land, pregnant with discontent; a land notorious for birthing a rebellious and prideful people who squabble like old hens and peck each other's eyes out over a kernel of corn?

Why should I waste my precious energy grappling with ancient and arcane interpretations of the meaning of life, when at this very moment my own life is quickly vanishing into an epic vapor? Why should I ponder over archaic events when current events nip at my heels, and today's revelations flash images of sweet and sensual chronicles in quantum leaps, whisking the guilt slate clean, merrily erasing the horrific mistakes of the distant and dreaded past?

Why should I embrace unconditionally one solitary man's independent view of the world; why should one individual's opinion be so elevated into the stratosphere, arrogantly advertised as the only
way; ramrodded through the bore of the universe as the singular and absolute truth? Why should one philosophical mandate be exclusive and rule over all, boldly claiming the title of undisputed champion of the world? Isn't there more than one way to "skin the cat?" Can't life be multiple choice? Can't life be more than a question of true and false? Can't we rightfully and responsibly come together and quibble over the definition of right and wrong?

These are some of the sentiments more popular today than ever before. They are the byproducts of a democratic society, when God is asked to step aside. They are also some of the very questions that inspired me to write this book. I write it as much or more for myself as I do for you, because I need a committee–free, personally crafted, truth-based, once-and-for-all-time, confident and coherent answer to these questions; and others like them. The answers to these questions are of critical importance to our future, both individually and collectively. Our response determines our destiny.

Modern man is living superficiously in a suspended reality, wondering who and what to believe, waiting and hoping the truth will soon magically emerge from all the chaos. So many conflicting voices have battled for his allegiance for so long that he has tuned them all out, putting his belief system on standby. He has grown content within his agnostic stalemate, content to postpone endless trivial confrontations and commitments.

Modern man lives day to day, disconnected from Eternity, flying by the seat of his pants, blowing in the wind, longing for absolutes but doubting their existence, like little boys fishing in a mud puddle.

Information overload is the latest cultural epidemic. It has produced an authority crisis. No one has earned our trust, consequently we trust no one, not even ourselves. The institutions we once trusted have betrayed us. Our political leaders lie to us boldly, openly and unashamedly; the media is no longer a trusted watchdog, but an ideological guard dog that barks incessantly up the wrong tree; our educational system is afflicted with relativism and has no sound basis on which to teach critical thinking skills, instead, they teach critical feeling skills; science and technology march to the tune of the highest bidder; the entertainment crowd is busy in bed with perversion and distortion and will stop at nothing to shock their audience of sex slaves; religion is marginalized, marinated and melted into the pluralistic pot as a social appetizer, as if all religions are equally tasty, or tasteless, depending on the taster. God is just another cog in series of secular wheels, hardly noticed until the machine grinds to a halt.

Many of our Christian leaders have grown weary with the enormous struggle against evil. They no longer have a taste for the fight. They lay prostrate, stubbornly root bound in their own tiny Garden of Gethsemane, too tired, too afraid or too lazy to rise up and unite with other Christians and proclaim the universal authority of Christ. Not thy will, but mine, they whimper.

The few who do rise up are gawked at like unicorns, even persecuted by their own people. Too many of our churches are mimicking the culture, hoping to attract an apathetic public by poking a compromised gospel down deep inside a sweet morsel that is easy to swallow, creating petty buffets for whiny bands of culture-bound baby Christians, tepid followers fueled by personal feelings and turned off by spiritual facts.

There is, fortunately, the remnant who always ignores the innuendos, insults, and indignities and braves the adversities to teach us by their very lives the whole truth and nothing but the truth. It is only and always through these courageous and committed souls that the Eternal words of Christ ring true, "I WILL BUILD MY CHURCH AND THE GATES OF HELL WILL NOT PREVAIL AGAINST IT!" The true Christian soldiers are always easily identifiable. Today, they are the ones singled out by the hate police and declared candidates for sensitivity training.

It is true that more and more church goers are choosing to stay home on Sunday morning. Some churches have closed their doors. The statistics all point to a decline in organized Christianity. Paradoxically, the true church is alive and well and growing. How can this be? I remember Billy Graham once saying that many people who attend church are not there for the right reason and most are unsaved. Since it is no longer cool to be a Christian, these cultural Christians are dropping out, purifying the church of much of its hypocrisy and allowing it to grow.

Jesus knows well the signs of the times. It was in times like ours when He Himself walked on earth. With all the advancements of mankind, two things have not changed—the unconditional and undying love of God for His people and the consistent, rebellious, disobedient nature of mankind. Mankind, despite all his proud advancement, still desires to please himself first, rather than the God who created him.

In Jesus' day, the Roman government had some similarities to our own-- bloated, self-centered and corrupt; the culture was immoral to the core; crime and poverty ran rampant throughout the land; superstition and witchcraft were prevalent; numerous philosophies and religions battled for the minds and hearts of men; the people were addicted to the "bread and circuses" the heroic government happily provided by shifting and saddling each and every possible burden to the aging and aching backs of the ever diminishing working class. Disaster was just ahead for them as it is for us.

It was in the midst of this degradation that Jesus boldly announced the only possible way out of the mess. For the people in His day, for the people in our day, or the people of all days, the message is the same—"Follow me...I am the way, the truth, and the life...there is no other way..." This solitary and exclusive declaration will never be amended to suit the whims of any man or movement.

Jesus will not force us to follow Him. Jesus did not, or will He ever, renounce our free will, He leaves it fully and daily intact, but He makes it abundantly clear that we have a choice to make, and it is left to each individual to make it. He does not force it upon us. You may bail out at any time along the way, but He does not offer multiple choices. He narrows all of the options down to two – 1) Go with Him, His way, or, 2) go your own way. There is no middle ground. Jesus said, "You cannot serve two masters...those who are not for me are against me."

Some continue to invent other options. What about Darwin and Deepak and Mohamed and Buddha and all those other boys with creative imaginations? Is Jesus sensitive to their ideas? They too have, or had, the same two options we have. Throughout the ages people have searched for alternative lifestyles more in line with their personal preference. Some defiantly, others unwittingly, seek to be their own God.

The overwhelming majority of each and every generation rejects Jesus; some condemning Him because He is too narrow, others condemning Him because He is too broad. Regardless of our individual talent in intellectual assessment, or our imaginative gift of emotional drivel, Jesus' response is always the same, "depart from me, I never knew you."

Consider briefly the option championed by disciples of Darwin, the father of the modern day Godless universe, whereby only those select few who survive the evolutionary processes of time and chance become suitable for the status of supreme and sovereign beings.

By evolution, I do not mean how certain organisms or species behave over time. I do not mean that all of it is bull because most of it is bull. By evolution, I mean the proposition which attempts to make a comprehensive explanation for all that is and how it got here. I mean that you do not have to accept totally what is only true partially. Because Darwin supposed a few answers to a few selected questions in no way means that he provided the ultimate answer to all questions.

By evolution, I mean more specifically, the highly imaginative speculation that some mysterious unknown, unnamed, and unexaminable inanimate substance appeared one historic day, by no particular means, for no apparent reason, from who knows where, or when; but having then appeared out of the wealth of nothingness, began to be influenced by stimuli and processes, which themselves had no reason to exist, but nevertheless, our mysterious suspect stumbled blindly onward, responding randomly and irrationally, and consequently growing ever more confident and stronger by the exposure to the unexplained forces.

In what way the strange substance grew stronger, and how, and why, I cannot tell, for there were no standard means yet available at that time by which to observe, analyze, investigate, measure, interview, or photograph the phenomenon. Neither can I provide insight as to the nature and origin of the forces that exercised influence upon our neo-substance. Nevertheless, in the fullness of time, and chance, which themselves had to originate from some unknown place, our unnamed substance makes a magical leap forward, from inanimate to animate, from death to life.

Mind you, time is the key here, as well as his partner, chance. Neither could pull it off alone, such a miraculous event requires two gods, not one. The necessity of going from nothing to something, and then from something to life, demands the pair working in tandem. Furthermore, it demands eons of time and truck loads of chance to make these impossible leaps. To hop and skip all the way from nothing to life is not something to sneeze at. Do not expect to achieve it, or unravel it in your lifetime, only Dr. Seuss could imagine it, and only the evolutionist can achieve it.

Time and chance; that is the secret explanation, and the only one you will ever get from the evolutionist; the same evolutionist who falls to his knees and laughs himself into a fit of hysteria because I believe in fairy tales; the same evolutionist who snarls at me for not acknowledging his superior grasp of the fundamentals of life, more specifically, his scholarly access to secret information which explains how the gods of time and chance operate; the same evolutionist who pours out all his pity on those of us who have not evolved enough to possess the elite ability to think like he does.

Eventually, in their own time and their own secret way, the scientific gods of time and chance force our mysterious substance into this remarkable metamorphosis. He had no choice about it; the greatness of evolution was thrust upon him. There are no choices with evolution, and no forgiveness, and no mercy.

Our suspect has now leaped from death to life by the grace of the gods of time and chance. Have faith in the experts, my friend, that is all you need to know, never mind the details at this incredible juncture. Remember, a human mind which has evolved over eons of time and chance has more experience and credibility, thus more capable of perfection than the simple mind with which you and I labor.

Do not trifle with questions like why the Dr. Spock-like mind of the evolutionist has progressed so much further along than our own, considering our minds are about the same age, give or take an eon or two. Just rest yourself securely in the fact that a mind designed and created in one sitting by a creator surely could not hold a light to a highly mutated mind which is growing closer and closer to perfection with every tick of the clock.

At this point in our journey back into the black holes of history, our mysterious substance is far enough along and distinguished enough that we can honor it with a name. Behold, the amoeba! Now that it has a name, the debate has ended. It is a well published fact that anything published by an evolutionist must be a fact, and anything that has a name must actually exist, particularly, when the poor thing has survived so many eons of trauma.

So, do not bother yourself anymore with half a million troubling details concerning how it all came together, we are beyond that now, wash it out of your mind, our substance now has existence, it is alive by declaration whether you like it or not, just accept it, and embrace it and celebrate the miraculous fact that you have discovered one of your many extremely elusive ancestors.

You must have respect for what the substance has been through and give credit where credit is due…remember, what billions of years ago existed as no more than a speck from nowhere and with no reputation has now come to life and distinguished itself with a name. And anything with a name has rights, which you must respect. Embrace progress. Where is your tolerance and compassion? Well…I suppose they are like mine–still evolving.

Do not grow weary in evolving, my friend, we are still a little ways from completing our journey. So far, we are only two leaps into our fantasy. Our suspect, having leaped brilliantly from nothing to something, and astonishingly hopping from death to life, shall presently petition the elite gods of time and chance for permission to make the last long jump from amoeba to man.

Now we are getting closer to home. Certainly, being this close to home we will begin to see things more familiar to us. Things like transitional fossils should be scattered all over the landscape as they have fought and died valiantly in the battle of survival for who knows what. What do you say? Not a single transitional fossil has been found anywhere in the world across the eons of time!

Are there no monuments, no grave stones, not even a single relic to commemorate the three greatest events in the history of the world—the miraculous leap from nothing to something, or the marvelous rise from death to life, nor the amazing hop from life to man? Never mind that little detail, have faith, press on, not enough time has passed; you must learn to trust the evolutionist, the appropriate fossils will appear in another eon or two.

I am aware that the journey is growing less and less fascinating, more routine, even mundane and monotonous. Actually, I am sick of it. My poor unreliable, partially-evolved mind is beginning to suspect that I will arrive at nowhere soon. I am beginning to sense the strong pungent odor of pessimism. The greater terror is that this vacuous pall of godless pessimism will be all I have to show for this sickening circular journey; that when I have reached the place where home ought to be, there will be the constant, cold, merciless, murderous mindset that there is no end to this madness, that only death can kill it, and even then, maybe not.

My poor partially-evolved mind is afflicted with the insane thought that even death will not release me from this madness. I suspect that if I were to buy this metaphysical madness lock, stock and barrel, the contract would require me to take it with me into Eternity. But, I have only evolved far enough to assume that the cannibalistic nature of atheism is exponentially insatiable; like cocaine, it requires more and more of its victims.

Regrettably, I must press on a little further, just a few more paragraphs. Having swallowed two, three hump camels already, why should I now stop and balk at the third and final one. To get ourselves from amoeba to man, a potentially complex and laborious journey, for the sake of time, we will take the quick route, the interstate, not the back roads where all the slow and snoopy drivers poke along.

Our amoeba finds himself lost in dark space, helpless, blind, deaf, dumb, and naked, surrounded by a vast, nameless and skeptical environment, and random conditions with the same credentials. But the good news is, the puny and pathetic amoeba has billions of years at its disposal, more time than it could ever need to turn into a man, even enough to turn into a computer, or, if the mutations are graceful, a turtle who can play Beethoven on the tuba.

One of the mysterious and unnamed environmental conditions which happened to attract our amoeba is a fluid-like substance, which billions of years later is suspected to be water, as it is so called today. Do not get sidetracked and concern yourself with where the water came from; Darwin had no biochemistry books to work with, just focus on the amoeba so we can get this over with.

As if it were preordained, which evolution strongly forbids, the water liked the amoeba and the amoeba liked the water. It may have been the very first example of "love at first sight" except for the fact that both were blind. Nevertheless, the amoeba, finally finding its natural habitat after eons of waiting patiently, naturally decided to learn to swim, though he did not know what swimming was, because he did not know what anything was; nevertheless, having learned to swim over the objection that he had nothing to swim with, or no genetic material to recommend the activity to him, the stubborn amoeba disregarded the circumstances and miraculously began to excel at the backstroke.

What swims in the water more often and more efficiently than a fish? And if it swims like a fish and behaves like a fish, then it deserves to be considered fishworthy. Thus, as you suspected, our amoeba is about to mutate another rung up the organizational ladder and is no longer destined to mull about in the mud like lowly amoebas are prone to do.

Behold, the fish! See how easily this new creature has broken free from its slimy cell of protoplasm, free also from the banal baggage of explanations, swimming proudly from its dim and obscure past, bringing with it a new world order and some startling amenities; accessories like fins, scales, gills, eyes, digestive, circulatory, nervous, skeletal, and muscular systems; and all other popular features that fill up big fat biology books that have no taste for history.

Speaking of fish stories, a reliable explanation of much of the evolutionary theory may rest in one I happen to recall. Once, while fishing with some undisclosed kinfolk, a handsome fish was caught. I personally witnessed the event, and though I was only a small child, I can recall the jubilation. The specimen was a largemouth bass and weighed in at nearly six pounds. The fish provided not only a thrill, but a meal, and I enjoyed the pair as much as the two other fishermen. At various intervals thereafter, the afore mentioned kinfolk would broadcast the event to a new audience, delightfully reviving the memory in my mind and allowing it the live on.

However, there was always one glaring discrepancy, which was sufficient for me to notice, namely, the fish always gained weight. The fish grew from six to seven pounds in just a few days, and by the end of the month was up to eight pounds, and last I remember, he had tipped the scales at twelve, and could have fed a crowd of five thousand. That I realize is quite a remarkable tale, as tales go, but it is nothing to the evolutionist, give him enough time and chance and he could parlay the bass into a brontosaurus.

This, I believe, is the most outstanding feature of the theory of evolution. And only the most imaginative applicants need to apply for admission to their society. You and I could never gain entry; we are too dull and boring.

For example, who would have dreamed that the fish we left backstroking a while back would grow legs and morph into some kind of aboriginal amphibian, which would crawl up in the bulrushes and lay some eggs, all of which would hatch out little amphibians year after year for millions years, until one historic day, one egg hatched out as the original ugly duckling. That duckling, without a mate, then proceeded to hatch, and hatch, and hatch until she, or he, hatched out something that favored a duckbill platypus.

My memory grows fuzzy at this evolutionary stage, and I am too weary to continue on this journey. I cannot bear to remember how many jumps we have yet to make to get from the duckbill platypus to our most recent ancestor, the monkey. My desire now is to exit this interstate and get as far as I can from this subject.

You are on your own for now, but remember, I am responsible for none of what I have written. It is not my fault. I am a victim; a victim to be pitied for the inferior mutations that are so tediously slow in bringing me up to standard. All my deficiencies must be piled up at the feet of the whirling and whizzing biochemical forces which comprise me. It is simply by random chance that I said what I said, and I am what I am.

*In the appendix please note two letters that I wrote to a new acquaintance who happened to be an atheist and a used car salesman. I do not mean to make any connection between his belief system and his career choice except to help explain the metaphor I used to personalize the communication. I included the letters simply because they help to summarize some of my thoughts on evolution.

"If the blind lead the blind"

MATTHEW 15:14

"If the blind lead the blind"

MATTHEW 15:14

Chapter 5

I remember a time when I was about ten years old, my mother announced that her old alarm clock had finally given up the ghost, and it was time to invest in a new one. With great optimism, I bid her to tarry until I had examined it, diagnosed its deficiency, and applied the appropriate remedy. She had a sly smile on her face as she handed me the lifeless corpse.

I threw myself into its resurrection with great enthusiasm. After all, the clock appeared to be a very simple machine with only a short hand, a long hand, and a few corresponding knobs and levers on the back. In no time, I had the cover off and began to lay hands on its internal working organs.

I gently pressed, and pried, and pushed on former moving parts. Nothing happened. I adjusted a few obvious stress points to make it more comfortable. Nothing happened. I surmised that the gears were stuck and just needed a little encouragement. I encouraged them with a screwdriver. They failed to respond affectionately. I decided that the poor creature was a little dry, so I anointed it with 3n1 machine oil. Still nothing happened.

I searched and found granddaddy's hammer and began a little tap dance on points of interest, like I had watched him tap on a lug nut that would not turn loose. In the fullness of time, the mainspring rebelled and launched itself off into space, followed by a covey of gears and brackets. By the time they reentered the earth's atmosphere my mother's sly smile had burst into howling laughter. Of course, I did not know how to put it all back together.

Not to be defeated, I rounded it all up in a shoe box and announced that I would complete the resurrection on the next rainy day. Of course, that was my juvenile way of trying to save face, and the clock quickly dismissed itself from my bucket list.

This is quite often how we find ourselves. When our lives fall apart, we do not know how to put it all back together. And soon, we realize that all the king's horses and all the king's men cannot put us together again. With machines like clocks, there are people who understand their design and function and can repair them. I often marvel at people who invent things, and those who can repair things when they become dysfunctional. These superior minds are even more amazing than the machines they create. It is on these minds I rely when I need assistance, if I can find them, and if I can afford them.

I also marvel that mankind with all his brilliance finds it nearly impossible to govern himself, or get along with his fellow man. When it comes to solving our personal difficulties and the difficulties of society, human beings have a consistent record of failure. G. K. Chesterton (1874-1936) was a keen observer of history. He reminds us, "the doctrine of original sin is the only philosophy empirically validated by the centuries of recorded history."

To whom, then, do we turn when the wheels of life fall off? Certainly, there are medical and psychiatric professionals who can help us individually, and there are various social, judicial and religious systems in place to help resolve our differences collectively, but even then, they are fallible and limited, no one remedy can be applied to every circumstance, and sometimes they do more harm than good.

Human beings are all different. Circumstances are all different. Dysfunctions are all different. And human beings are a million times more complicated than a clock, consequently much more difficult to "fix". In fact, it is as likely that one man can totally fix another man as it is that one clock can fix another clock.

From a purely human perspective, it is difficult to even find a pulse on some of humanity's worst offenders. We have too many unique, delicate, and intricate parts and an array of varying experiences. No one person can fully understand another person. Many people have tried to fix me, but they all got frustrated and eventually gave up.

There is an old story I heard years ago which could be true, but if not, it is still a good story. It seems that a wealthy businessman had just bought himself a brand new Model T Ford. He had nearly arrived home when it broke down. He did not know how to fix it. He began to flag down every passerby until he had been through a dozen or so who could not fix it either. Eventually, an old man drove by and stopped. He took one look under the hood, made a minor adjustment to something totally unfamiliar to all the others. The car started right up. The wealthy man was astonished. He asked the old man, "how were you able to fix it when nobody else could?" The old man replied, "My name his Henry Ford, sir, I invented it."

I believe that human beings have an inventor, or more appropriately, a Creator, who created us in His image. He designed all the components. He knows all our individual parts and how they work together. He knows not only how to fix us individually; He knows how to fix the whole bunch of us. He knows how to straighten out this gigantic mess we find ourselves in today. He has provided us an owner's manual, which we invariably do not read. Perhaps it is time to wipe the dust from it and see what it says.

The God of the Bible is a God of harmony and peace and order. It is historically verifiable that the closer a society adheres to the written Word of God, the more harmony and peace and order they experience; and the further away they go from His laws, the more chaotic the world becomes.

Why is it so hard for some people to accept the simple concept of a singular Creator God? Why is it so easy for others? God says that in both cases the answer resides in the individual hearts of men. God created the heart of man with powerful discretionary abilities. Some are instinctive, others are analytical, and others are even beyond our ability to comprehend. They combine to give us the ability to make proper choices. In essence, we were all hard wired to hear the voice of our Creator.

Adam and Eve were the first to pervert these God-given attributes. They were not given ten commandments. They were given one. This singular command left them with two simple options—choose to obey God, or choose to disobey God. Interestingly, we all have the same two options today.

They were both challenged, or tempted, in different ways. Eve's femininity was challenged by the serpent to doubt God's goodness, as if God, or maybe her husband, was holding out on her. Satan, disguised as a serpent, cleverly approached Eve first, calculating that Adam, being the original human, would have never doubted God's goodness.

The serpent believed that Adam required a different style and kind of deception. He reasoned correctly that Adam needed a more masculine challenge, that Adam would be more easily seduced by his own wife, sensing it was his duty to protect her best interest. Adam had his own doubts, as we all do. He doubted God's power. He doubted that God could fix the mess his wife had created. How clever of Satan to tailor each temptation to suit the subject. He is still doing it today. He knows what tempts me may not work for you. But he is carefully watching us all to see what our particular weaknesses are.

God's Word quickly teaches us the distinction between good and evil. From a human perspective, good may be defined simply as obedience to God, and evil as disobedience to God. From a divine perspective, there is no good outside of God. God alone is good, everything and everyone else falls short of His goodness. Any belief system or any moral law that falls outside the declarations of God is therefore evil.

There is much more to learn about the distinction between the good and evil. Jesus liked to use the analogy of light and dark. In the same way that darkness is the absence of light, so evil is the absence of good. Good, then, is somewhat of a partial synonym for God, and evil a perfect synonym of anti-God. These definitions and explanations paint a clear picture of God as absolute with no room for theories of relativity as it relates to Christian morality.

In this way, Jesus enlightens us as to the stark inequality between good and evil. Evil can be further understood as an assault against the truth. Evil is a lie masquerading as truth. Evil is pretense, something pretending to be what it is not. Therefore, good and evil are not opposites as some would have us believe. Evil can never be considered as something on the same level as good. Evil, in fact, owes its very existence to good, and would not exist without it.

Evil was never a thing created. It originated as an alternative to good. Having no way to support itself, evil must attach itself to good like a parasite, like a tick sucks its life force from the blood of its host. Evil, therefore, must be clearly classified as a something counterfeit, a fake that portrays itself as real. Evil can be further described as a deviation, or a distortion, or a perversion of good which may begin as a slight, pale shade of grey, then, gradually grows darker and darker until it reaches the pitch black blindness of a moonless midnight.

Evil, because of its dark nature, can effectively blind a man to the things of God. The ultimate ambition of Satan, knowing he cannot eclipse God, is to spread enough evil to destroy God's creation, particularly His people. This reveals the idiotic arrogance of the useful idiots who Satan recruits to do his dirty work, who think they are doing the world a favor by persecuting Christians, who in essence gnaw on the hand that feeds them, who in their brilliance of devising devilish schemes against God, never seem to realize that they are trying to destroy the very source of their existence. "The fool has said in his heart, there is no God." How a man who says he does not believe in God can fight so vigorously against the God in whom he does not believe is a mystery to me, the very apex of hypocrisy.

In addition to powers of discretion, God designed every one of us with the freedom to choose our own response to the circumstances we encounter. God saw fit to leave certain critical decisions up to us. You and I can hardly fathom the power in this gift, and the responsibility. This exceptional gift, the gift of free will, gives every human being the option to choose good or evil, to chose even to deny the very God who created us. Adam and Eve, knowing well enough what was good, chose evil. Consequently, every human being thereafter inherited the propensity. That is the bad news.

The good news is that every human being also inherited the innate ability to sense when we are wrong. St. Augustine stated that we were created with "a God-shaped vacuum in our hearts" and we are unable to rest until we find rest in God. Essentially, though not identically, we all have the same choice and the same equipment Adam and Eve had. And, just as Adam and Eve, we will be tempted by Satan to choose incorrectly.

The better news is that every evil heart, no matter how evil, can be redeemed and restored and transformed into good. We need not be held responsible for the original sin, or held in bondage for the sins of our parents, or our fellow man, or even our own. Though each is accountable only for his own sin, those too can be erased by the Grace of God.

However, man himself does not possess the power to perform the transformation; God alone has to perform it. God is in charge of forgiveness. Man is in charge of repentance. Man can only submit to the authority of God and grant Him permission to perform the operation.

Obviously, when I speak of the heart, I am not speaking of the physical organ that pumps blood, but the spiritual essence that includes the mind, the emotions, the will and all the invisible components that comprise an individual. I once composed a little poem to help me understand why I am so enticed by evil. I entitled it:

"THE ORIGIN OF WAR"
The origin of war can be traced,
to the color red in Cain's cold face;
Since that day the truth holds fast,
the mold then formed, the die then cast;
Man's desire to master his fate,
declared himself potentate.

It is the greatest desire of every man to be free from all authority. We do not want anybody telling us what to do. Cain did not want to the held to a higher standard than he chose for himself. Though he was fully aware of the existence of God, he, like his parents, rejected God's authority over Him. He saw God as a hindrance to his freedom, as someone who got in the way of what he wanted to do. This, in a nutshell, is the basic problem with all mankind. We are not content with the image. We want to be our own God. We want to make our own rules.

It is highly likely that Cain blamed his parents, just as his father blamed his mother, and his mother blamed the serpent. It runs in the family. If not his parents, then Cain blamed God himself for making him the way he was. The origin of victimhood began in the first family. It still reigns today, handed down over the centuries, as the most popular, readily available and worn out excuse for a man to deny his free will, and his personal responsibility, and blame someone else for his own sin.

Our modern day society promotes personal irresponsibility by claiming that man is by nature good but is corrupted by his heredity and or his environment. This is the gigantic foundational error that is responsible for the chaos that exists in the world today. It has undermined the divine order of all things. This single systemic defect has created an easy way out for all wrong doers by relieving them from any accountability, giving them an overarching excuse for all their failures.

This singular systemic defect has evolved into an elaborate system of ever expanding conundrums that creates hordes of victims who blame all their deficiencies on anybody or anything but themselves. If not acknowledged and corrected it will decimate future generations. Be sure, man is not good by nature, but evil! Only God is good and only God can redeem man.

Cain became angry over a feeling that he falsely perceived to be a fact; a feeling that he was being unfairly punished for what his parents did. He was clearly jealous of his brother Abel, who had the same sinful parents, but humbly respected the authority of God. Again, we find ourselves going back to the individual heart of humans. Abel's heart was right with God. Cain's was not. Cain alone was responsible for his consequences, in like manner, so are we. The principle of sowing and reaping runs threadlike through all our lives.

Adam and Eve accepted their punishment and moved on, however, Cain, a second generation sinner, took it to another level. He allowed his anger, resentment and jealousy to run him hot with rage. And he rose up and killed the closest person he could get his hands on, his own brother, who had done no wrong.

God's Word warns us that sin over time grows more and more diabolical. James 1:15 reminds us, "then, after desire has conceived, it gives birth to sin, and sin, when it is full grown, gives birth to death." Death is the inevitable result of sin. People sin because they are sinners at heart, people kill physically because they are dead spiritually. It is when sin is allowed to go unchecked and reaches full maturity that the most horrendous acts of man occur. In this case, it was an innocent man who died at the hands of his own brother, a wicked brother with no regard for anyone but himself.

Jesus has the ability to see into every person's heart through all dimensions of time–past, present and future. He sees the vast chronological march of all mankind as a single snapshot. This unique attribute qualifies Him to be the perfect judge of all humanity. No one goes to Heaven or hell until Jesus makes the call, thus making certain the decision is absolutely correct. Nobody slips through the cracks or sneaks in the back door. We can be certain that everyone is rightly judged.

Jesus is not only God in perfection; He is man in perfection. This makes Him not only the perfect judge, but the perfect role model, an attribute no other individual has ever, or will ever, possess. When Jesus walked on earth, He knew well who His enemies were. By the middle of the gospel of Matthew, Jesus had reached the peak of his popularity. He was well received by the poor and needy, loved by most of the common people, but He provoked anger and resentment and jealousy in the hearts of the religious leaders.

The Pharisee's and the elite religious leaders hated Jesus, very much like Cain hated his brother Abel, and very much for the same reason. Cain knew that his brother Abel was a righteous man, and he hated him for it. Jealousy is among the oldest excuses for evildoers. The Pharisees so desired to discredit Jesus that they assigned an entourage of spies and informants to follow him around to keep an eye on him and badger him at every opportunity. Matthew 15 brings into focus one of the many times Jesus squared off with his most persistent enemy–the Pharisees:

"Then some of the Pharisees and teachers of the law came to Jesus from Jerusalem and asked, 'Why do your disciples break the tradition of the elders? They don't wash their hands before they eat.'

Jesus replied, 'And why do you break the command of God for the sake of your tradition? For God said, Honor your father and mother and anyone who curses his father and mother must be put to death. But you say that if a man says to his father or mother, whatever help you might otherwise have received from me is a gift devoted to God. He is not to honor his father with it. Thus you nullify the word of God for the sake of your tradition. You hypocrites! Isaiah was right when he prophesied about you:

These people honor me with their lips,

But their hearts are far from me.
They worship me in vain;
Their teachings are but rules taught by men.'

Jesus called the crowd to him and said, 'Listen and understand, what goes into a man's mouth does not make him unclean, but what comes out of his mouth, that is what makes him unclean.' Then the disciples came to him and said, 'Do you know that the Pharisees were offended when they heard this?' He replied, 'Every plant that my heavenly Father has not planted will be pulled up by the roots. Leave them; they are blind guides. If a blind man leads a blind man, both will fall into a pit.'"

The disciples were stunned when they saw the way Jesus spoke of and to the Pharisees. The reason they were stunned is because it was stunning. It was beyond stunning. It was shocking, considering the centuries a preferential status the religious leaders had enjoyed. They were the respected leaders of the Jewish nation for centuries, no unlearned, illegitimate Jewish peasant like Jesus was even allowed to approach them, much less show the slightest hint of disrespect.

Moreover, the disciples were disturbed that Jesus offended the Pharisees by blatantly and publicly referring to them as hypocrites and blind guides. Furthermore, Jesus issued the ultimate insult when He instructed the crowd to ignore their teaching. I sense from Matthew's narrative that the disciples were somewhat offended themselves and may have cringed with fear at Jesus' overt and unapologetic attack. The disciples were Jews themselves and were still bound up in Jewish tradition. They had followed the Jewish traditions since birth. Years of traditional thought and corresponding behavior are not easy to dismiss, even for a disciple.

It appears that the disciples considered the provocation unwarranted and unnecessary, that Jesus had made a serious mistake. Certainly the tongue-lashing seemed out of character for Jesus and did not seem to help His cause. It appears that the disciples felt that Jesus should issue the Pharisees an apology. Of course, knowing Jesus like they did, they did not hold their breath until one was issued.

In our own lives, the sovereignty of God often offends us and can be easily interpreted as a little bit rude, and at other times, extremely harsh. Like the Pharisees, we sometimes get our feelings hurt and our tender hearts broken, and we too feel like Jesus owes us an apology, or at least, an explanation. Of course, I am yet to read in my Bible where the Son of God ever apologized to anybody for anything.

We are all bound up in our own limited experience and cannot help but look at Jesus through sentimental eyes and faulty human logic. That is the reason we are perplexed by the paradoxes He presents us. Everything He said and did had a perfect Eternal perspective. We operate from a defective earthly perspective. We expect a certain earthy consistency from Jesus, which turns out to be an extremely narrow minded and superficial consistency based solely on our personal experience. As Anais Nin reminds us, "we don't see things as they are, we see them as we are."

The disciples saw what they thought was an inconsistency between Jesus' teaching and His actions. He taught his disciples not only to love their neighbor, but to love their enemies, and to pray for them, to forgive them seven times seventy, to turn the other cheek, and to go the second mile. Now, Jesus appears to be miles away from His own teaching. Gentle Jesus, meek and mild, has seemingly lost His religion.

If we fast forward to Matthew 23 and read the chapter in context, we are even more astonished. Humble Jesus unleashes an unprecedented verbal assault on the so-called religious leaders, calling them every name in the book, names such as "blind fools... whitewashed tombs... snakes... a brood of vipers." To make matters worse, in the holy city of Jerusalem, and on the holiest time of the year, and on at least two occasions, Jesus took up a whip and ran the money changers out of the temple in a violent burst of righteous indignation.

So how do we reconcile such an inconsistency in the life of Jesus? How do we explain a man of peace acting so violently? Is He fighting fire with fire, evil with evil? Wasn't the essence of His message to fight evil with good? Did He let His emotions get the best of Him? Was He subject to the same mood swings as you and I? Is Jesus a God of love and grace, or is He a God of justice and judgment?

No, He is not fighting fire with fire, no, He did not allow His emotions to control Him, but yes, He is a God of love and grace, and also a God of justice and judgment. How could God be otherwise? Maybe we can all agree it is wrong to allow the wrongdoer to continue to do wrong when we have both the power and the responsibility to stop it. It is also wrong to allow the wrong doer to think he will suffer no consequences for his wrong doing?

Though evil may prevail for a time, Absolute Goodness intervenes when its purpose is accomplished. In due time, we all reap what we sow. Neither will Absolute Goodness whitewash evil? The wrath of man never produces the righteousness of God. It is the righteousness of God that produces righteousness in man. Whether repentance is produced by wrath or by grace, the salvation of men's souls is the end result. And God knows best which to apply and when.

Jesus is the ultimate paradox, the supernatural blending of God and man in one person. Jesus is one hundred per cent God and one hundred per cent man. He is the perfect paradox who never once sinned, who never once said something He should not have said, or did something He should not have done. Famous bible scholar, G. Campbell Morgan (1863-1945) brings us closer to understanding Jesus' relationship with the Pharisees:

"In these (Jesus') words there is a revelation of His passion for righteousness, and also of His compassion for the worst and most degraded. His passion for righteousness never destroys His compassion for the worst. His compassion for the worst never destroys His passion for righteousness. It is well that our hearts should be warned by these solemn woes. The work of the King is not the work of excusing a man who persists in unrighteousness, and presently admitting him to the presence of God and the heaven of light… if he must pronounce doom it will be with tears, but it will be pronounced."

Another way of stating the predicament is to say that facts should always override feelings. The fact was that Jesus' ministry on earth was about to end and the Pharisees had not yet heeded numerous previous warnings to repent. This was the crux of the matter. Time was running out, their chance for salvation nearly gone. They were well on their way to hell unless Jesus could provoke them into repentance by exposing their vile sin.

We will never fully understand all that Jesus is or how and why He does what He does, but we learn from the scriptures who He is not. He is not a warm and fuzzy love child who tolerates our favorite sin. He is not a happy curb hop who delights at fulfilling our every desire. He does not allow us to redefine what sin is. He is the Son of God who came to take away the sins of the world. He is the potter, we are the clay.

Jesus' last words in Matthew 23 express perfectly His reason for the provocation: "O Jerusalem, Jerusalem, you who kill the prophets and stone those sent to you, how often I have longed to gather your children together, as a hen gathers her chicks under her wings, but you were not willing. Look, your house is left desolate. For I tell you, you will not see me again until you say, 'Blessed is he who comes in the name of the Lord.'"

"No man having drunk old wine desireth new"

LUKE 5:39

"No man having drunk old wine desireth new"

LUKE 5:39

Chapter 6

Jim Reeves (1923-1964) was an exceptional baseball player in high school. He was so exceptional as a pitcher, that he received an athletic scholarship to the University of Texas. It was there that he severed his sciatic nerve and shattered his dream of playing in the major leagues. He turned to music and song writing and became known as "Gentleman Jim," the man with the velvet voice.

He sang "Welcome to My World", which opened the door for us to enjoy his style of easy listening music. Many of us found him welcome in our world as he began to release hit after hit; hits like: "I Can't Stop Loving You"; "Put Your Sweet Lips A Little Closer To The Phone"; "Make The World Go Away." He was certainly a welcomed addition to the country music of that day and time.

In my opinion, he is still a delightful alternative to what we are hearing this day and time. We sang along with Gentleman

Jim as we skated to his music as teenagers in the old Pelham, Georgia skating rink. What a handsome memory that is.

Tragically, Gentleman Jim was killed in a plane crash just outside of Nashville, Tennessee, the summer I graduated from high school, 1964. He was only forty years old. He had a world of music left in him, and we were all broken hearted that he never got to sing it.

It was about that time when the world I grew up in began to change. New ideologies began to rise up and challenge the old. The creative arts are always the first to recognize and express the most subtle forms of change. The Beatles caught on, and The Rolling Stones, then the rest of the rock and roll clan followed suit. It was then and there that the hippie, yippie, yuppie, and yappie revolution was born in America.

Like a new born baby, the hope of a brand new lifestyle blossomed into a delightful novelty, an exciting sub-cultural alternative for the cool and cavalier baby boomer generation. It was a liberating breath of fresh air, an overdue break from the boring lifestyle that our old foggied parents and grandparents had advertised for generations.

We thought at the time that we were just merrily "rolling on the river" like "Proud Mary," everybody doing their own thing, living life to its fullest, grabbing all the gusto we could along the way. We thought at the time that we were not bothering or hurting anyone, just expressing our new found freedoms with brave new lifestyles.

However, a new born baby brings with it new priorities and responsibilities of which we were tragically ignorant, and in most cases, apathetic. Ignorance and apathy are two of the great curses of mankind. When individual rights are exalted without the restraint of responsibility, the common bonds of humanity disintegrate. When liberty is unleashed without boundaries, humanity quickly lapses into chaos. The law of compensation can never be amended, there are no exceptions. Sooner or later, we all face consequences. Sooner or later we all have to pay the fiddler.

Each generation must deal with change; none more so, in recent times, than my own. We have witnessed our novel and fresh breath of liberation mutate into an addictive and enslaving evil. What originally began in hope has morphed into despair. Gradually at first, but progressively growing more viral, the greedy contagion has now reached epidemic stage. This reckless shift in values has now overwhelmed and over burdened a society so unaware and unconcerned that nothing short of absolute repentance can save it.

How could such a catastrophe have occurred a single generation? How could we have abandoned the very values that propelled us into unprecedented prosperity? Simply stated, a society disintegrates in the degree that it removes the spiritual absolutes that support its moral foundation. More simply stated, when we give up on God, we go to hell in a hurry!

Coming to our senses, many of us "boomers" have just recently put out the anchor and are trying to restart the motor and travel back upstream. We are wondering how we got so far from home and if we have drifted too far downstream; we are wondering if we have enough time to make it back to solid ground, back to the Rock on which our parents homesteaded; back to the home place; back before we wandered into the land of prodigals.

We realize now, that from that stable and hallowed position, we can better guide those who come after us. We would love to see our new world rebuilt upon the old Rock, rather than this shifty sand we are now sinking in. We wonder if it is too late.

Unfortunately, it is too late for some. Some of our friends won't make it back, some left this world before they planned to; some are still stoned and oblivious to anything but their addiction; some remain apathetic; others are defeated and have given up the fight. Some don't want to go back, and some of those, a small perverted minority, fight violently against going back. They call themselves "progressives." They don't believe in absolutes, they see traditional values as a digression, an infringement upon their ever expanding human rights.

The journey back will be uphill; it will be tedious and treacherous, but it will be much harder and much longer if we keep sliding down this sand hill. Hard as it may be, I am certain some of us will make it; God will see to it that we do; He always has His remnant; but it is doubtful that we will all make it. Even so, I hope we can soon awaken enough to revive and redeem our nation.

Some people see the problems we face today simply as generational differences. They believe that when all us old fogies die off their utopian dream will magically appear. That is a totally inept and disastrous diagnosis. The problems we face are much deeper than generational differences. Our problems are not about what is old and what is new. Our problems are about what is right and what is wrong, and more specifically–who gets to define what is right and what is wrong. Contemporary America has an authority problem. We have foolishly elected culture as the ultimate authority.

Taking a short journey back into my personal history will help to explain what I mean. I was born in 1946. It was generally a happy time. Soldiers were returning from World War II victorious. Thousands of soldiers quickly went to work repopulating the nation. The sudden surge in childbirths created a lifelong nickname for my generation– "baby boomers."

Presently, I am considered an elder in that generation. We are beginning to die off. In a few decades, most of us will be extinct. One of the distinctions many elders possess is a deep and abiding affinity for the generation that raised us—the "traditionalist." They are sometimes called "the greatest generation" because they never compromised their ideals despite the harshness of the Depression and the tragic toll of war. Though most of them are gone, the severe sacrifices they made and the mental and physical toughness they displayed can never be erased from our memories.

Many of my generation are more endeared to that generation than to our own. In our younger years, we protested their strict adherence to structure and we rebelled against their hard-nosed and disciplined approach to life; but today, many of us prodigals have cycled back to it and re-embraced their mind set. Many of us eventually came to respect the reason for it and the value in it, and we are hoping we can preserve the remnants of it for our children and grandchildren. Over the long haul, we have confirmed our spiritual suspicions—that what we once considered as infringements upon our freedom was in reality our very best protection against evil.

Most of my heroes come from that generation. So heroic were they that I sometimes express a general disappointment in my own generation. Under the tough exterior of that no-nonsense generation was a mammoth sense of personal responsibility. It was their driving force. Everyone had to carry their own weight.

In those days, a person was defined by their work ethic. A man who would not work was a disgrace. It was considered shameful to accept charity. I often groaned in despair when my parents made me return the fifty cents given me for doing a favor for my elderly neighbor.

Baby-boomers begrudgingly inherited the traditional attitude toward work. Most of us had little to say in the matter. We were hammered daily with the obvious link between success and hard work. We were also hammered with the value of education. Our parents wanted us to have more opportunities than they did, and they saw education as the way to get it.

An education was something that no one could take away from you, and it would provide you with the essentials of making a living. Consequently, you would never have to depend on someone else. Self-reliance was the highest of ideals.

Education was not a social experiment. It was highly structured around reading and writing and math skills. It was teacher centered. There was very little interaction between teacher and student. The teacher lectured and you paid attention. The teacher assigned work and you performed it without question or complaint. Discipline was held in high esteem. Class disruptions were not tolerated. Corporal punishment was available on demand both at school and at home. Home and school were cut out of the same fabric, one complimenting the other.

Teachers were not schooled in learning styles, self-image psychology, moral relevance, social engineering, or student's rights. My personal feelings and dysfunctions were woefully irrelevant to all my teachers, and my juvenile opinions and excuses had to stand at the back of a long line of historical facts. Character education was built in to each lesson.

Once you finished high school you had three choices: 1) further your education through college or technical school, 2) go to the military, or 3) go to work. There were no safety nets or free lunches. The work ethic carried over into which of the three you chose. You were expected to move quickly from consumer to producer. In employee/employer relationships, we were taught to be grateful for the opportunity, however menial it was.

Work was defined as an opportunity, and with diligence and initiative you could work your way up. Loyalty to the employer was expected, a full day's work for a full day's pay. Honesty was the best policy. A man's word was his bond. You were expected to own up to your mistakes, learn from them, and not blame someone else for them. Many, if not most of my friends, selected a career early in life and never deviated from it, investing forty or more diligent years in the same work.

Ironically, it was in my pursuit of higher education in the 1960's when he winds of change began to blow for the "boomer" generation; and ultimately for the rest of the nation. There were a number of events that ushered in radically new generational conflicts, and there was a new ideologue poised and ready to exploit each new crisis.

The assassination of John F. Kennedy opened our eyes to the evil that lived among us. The Viet Nam War confirmed that there was evil all around us. The violence of campus protests and the civil rights movement unmasked the evil that lived within us. Activists and rebels along with their friends in the media discovered they could influence legislation and began to apply pressure at every opportunity. Unrest became the new status quo, ultimately provoking the people to mistrust anyone in authority, and eventually, anyone with a different world view.

The shade tree activist, who is generally oblivious to the consequences of his actions, found himself daily before the camera. Intoxicated by his illegitimate and unwarranted celebrity, he began to consider himself credible, and even heroic. He focused his wrath upon what his narrow mind told him was the matter with humanity. He determined that inequality was the root of all evil.

Divisions in race, religion, gender, ethnicity, socio-economic status and ideologies illuminated the landscape. Sociology based on perception became the new battlefield. Some of the protests had legitimate merit and motive and were long overdue. Certainly, there is always merit in rectifying injustice. When God given rights are denied, the entire world should rise up and protest.

But, the legitimate movements were soon hijacked by every crackpot whose forte was smoking pot, tripping on LSD, singing and painting psychedelic art, and living parasitically off someone else's dime. The tares grew abundantly amidst the wheat as tares always do.

The greedy menagerie with the help of a sympathetic media grew into a monstrosity which soon exceeded the powers of government as an agent for change. Activist after activist found a bumper and jumped on until the parade filled Main Street, flooded into the suburbs, and fanned out electronically into the tiniest living rooms in America. Ninety percent of the nation, working daily to make a living, silently revolted against the irresponsible ten cent leading the colorful parade.

The sexual revolution saw its opportunity to jump on board and ride the crest of the wave. What had been private and sacred became public and secular, what previously hid in back street alleys, joined the parade down Main Street. The smugly righteous and the blatantly unrighteous rode in the same vehicle and slept in the same bed. Sex soon replaced apple pie as the great American appetizer.

First, sex advertised itself, then, reveling in its illegitimate glory, rose up to advertise everything else. Today, nothing sells that isn't sexy. Mysteriously, in the midst of the sexual revolution, little children stranded in the womb by perverted and unrestrained sexual appetites lost their voice among the activists.

Their unheard voices are still today the most unsung, and most unequal in all the world. The grandiose plans of the modern day activist, to make the world a better place, presses forth in the name of tolerance and inclusion. But his hypocritical and crony commitment to tolerance does not include anyone who might challenge his view of the world.

The permissiveness, which produced promiscuity, promoted mistrust among the sexes. Rising divorce rates put both parents to work leaving children to fend for themselves. Children learned mistrust and the art of deception before they learned their ABC's.

The loosening of traditional values released more and more inhibitions, making experimental drug use more fashionable. The moral foundation that the traditional generation prized so highly began to crack under the combined speed and weight of rapid reform. Character traits such as loyalty, honesty, and trust were drawn into battle with more pragmatic solutions. Situational ethics became the calling card of the great elite problem solvers.

By the 1970's, the settled ways of the older generation was forced to share time and space with budding progressive approaches. Long standing practices merged with experimentation. In schools, learning styles became popular. Institutions of higher learning began to magnify diversity. Government funded experiments in social engineering became the answer to all our problems. The attempt to educate the masses with a clearly defined, content based curriculum and strategy began to give way. In due time, the rigorous demands of academic achievement was tempered by a softer self-image psychology. Socialization demanded equal time with academics.

A student's educational experience focused as much on feelings as on facts, and more dangerously, on perception as much as reality. Substance had to make room for style. The media became addicted to perception and took every opportunity to promote the kinder, gentler, stylish mentality of the newcomers.

Over the years, the progressive approach to education became the norm, naturally spilling over into the workplace and seeping into the fabric of society. The powers to be were fully aware of the proverb, "change the youth and you change the nation." As a result, younger generations became more conditioned to change and more willing to accept it, whether it was good, bad, or indifferent. Change for the sake of change became as popular as the change that actually makes things better. Critical thinking skills were no longer necessary because someone was always there to tell you what and how to think.

The values that the traditional generation held as absolutes were on the wane, wearied by the constant blind-sided attacks by every new whim of relativism. Relativism naturally fell in love with rhetoric, got married and birthed political correctness. By the time the 1990's rolled around, we no longer knew the definition of "is."

It is natural to expect change and to welcome it when it brings progress. But all change does not bring progress. It is natural to expect differences in the thoughts and actions of various generations. It is natural to expect older generations to resist change, and younger generations to embrace it. Obviously that has been the trend.

It is not exceptionally difficult for society in general to process and successfully integrate gradual change, particular when it is based on wisdom and tested and found to be reliable. However, the radical changes of the last decade have transpired at such an overwhelming pace that there is much skepticism even among the young concerning the merit of change itself. Consequently, conflict between ideologies as well as generations has been more severe.

The ever growing demand to meet the needs and desires of a diverse and expanding population will only grow greater. Rapid change in science and technology and methodology are growing in quantum leaps. Rapidly evolving philosophies and world views are causing great paradigm shifts in the way human beings think and behave. As a contemporary society, we have been amazingly naive in reviewing and evaluating what we are changing and why.

New ideologies naturally emerge and challenge the old. In the presence of every new challenge, we will do well to remember that the complexities of life transcend generational differences, that the monumental tasks before us will require the best efforts of all generations, as well as all races, religions, genders, ethnicities, socio-economic status, and ideologies.

We will do well to acknowledge that the general difference between generations is far less significant than the vast and specific difference between individual world views. In the midst of unprecedented change, we must acknowledge that one thing does not change–the truth transcends generational differences. It is critical that we accurately define what is absolute.

We find highly talented and motivated individuals in all generations, just as well as we find the lazy and apathetic. In all generations, we find unyielding individuals stuck in their ways, refusing to change; and we find as well those so addicted to change that the very thrill and novelty of something new and different obscures the fact that unwise and untested changes usually spell disaster.

It is good to keep in mind that everything new is not necessarily good, nor is everything old necessarily bad. In the words of G.K. Chesterton, "before we tear down fences, we should figure out why they were put there in the first place."

I need not limit this brief historical analysis to my generation, or that of my parents and grandparents. I recall Gentleman Jim Reeves taking us back much further. I recall him singing, "Gimme That Old Time Religion…if it's good enough for the Hebrew children, it's good enough for me." It always seemed to me that there had to be considerably more significance in the age of a particular religion than was generally acknowledged. There is a reason some things endure and ultimately outlive others.

I have often wondered why people who talk about religion avoid talking about its origin. It seems to me that everybody is content to start in the middle. Nobody wants to start from the beginning. It may be startling to some and enlightening to others to consider the birthdays of the world's major religions.

I suspect that the original religion is likely the only true religion, and that all the others are derivatives. I suspect that any religion that came after the original was, at best, a spin off, an offshoot, a copycat, a Johnny come lately, or a wannabe; and, at worse, a deception, or a perversion. Certainly, the original is singular in nature and related to real time. All we have to do is find which one is the oldest and we have the original.

I have come to believe, like Jim Reeves, that what he called the "old time religion" is the original. Taking a very brief look back through history at the chronology of the five major world religions, we find a great difference in age. The youngest was born around 600 A.D., when Muhammad began to receive visions and hear voices, subsequently translating his singular experience into what is known today as Islam. Never mind that his first impression was that the visions and voices came from Satan.

Next, over a thousand years older, comes Buddhism, when Siddhartha Gautama, around 600 B.C., grew disillusioned with Hinduism and conceived what he thought was a better idea.

Next, traveling way backwards in history to 1400 B.C. we find Hinduism. There we find why Siddhartha became so disillusioned. Hinduism has a very elusive origin. It has no particular founder or anyone to explain its mysterious complexities.

From here, we go back another six hundred years to around 2000 B.C., where we find a man named Abraham, who God promised would be the father of a great nation, thus establishing the national religion of Judaism .

Then, finally, we arrive at what I refer to as the original, the only one which provides a plausible and comprehensive explanation of where we came from, where we are going, and why we are here.

The gospel of John describes it this way: "In the beginning was the Word, and the Word was with God, and the Word was God. He was with God in the beginning." (John 1:1-2 NIV) Who was with God in the beginning? Jesus was with God in the beginning. Jesus himself stated, "before Abraham was, I am!" (John 8:58)

Though many date the birth of Christianity at or around 30 A.D., that date simply references the thirty years or so that Jesus appeared on earth in the flesh. He appeared quite often long before that. Possibly, his first appearance was to comfort Hagar who was pregnant with Abraham's child. (Genesis 16:7)

It has been my intent to simply acknowledge the time line of the five major world religions, and not to compare or contrast the substance of each. There are libraries full of such discussions by authors much more qualified.

I return now to finish with the verse with which I began, "no man having drunk old wine desireth new." (Luke 5:39) To whom was Jesus speaking? He was speaking to the Pharisees. What was the essence of his message? His message was that people tend to prefer what taste good to them, or what is comfortable to them, or to what they have become accustomed. Jesus, in this parable, was the new wine, the Messiah, the one they had been looking for, but they rejected Him because He did not meet their specifications.

In reality, Jesus was the oldest of wine, having existed before Creation, but the Pharisees just could not stretch their minds back that far. In reality, we should not be overly concerned with what is old and what is new, but we should be extremely concerned with what is false and what is true.

"Beware of false prophets"

MATTHEW 7:15

"Beware of false prophets"

MATTHEW 7:15

Chapter 7

A friend of mine asked me one day, "how do you KNOW you are a Christian?" I immediately sensed in him the twinkle of anticipation. He was hoping I would say, "because I believe in Jesus." Then, he could quote me the famous verse, James 2:19, "...even the devil believes in Jesus...." But, I had been to the woodshed a few times already by that same line, and miraculously, I had learned from my mistake, which is my customary way of learning. I was aware of his little trick. To his chagrin, I did not take the bait.

Instead, I said, "I KNOW I am a Christian because I am a FOLLOWER of Jesus," though I had to admit that I wander off from time to time. The devil surely is a believer, but not a follower. Obedience is the key. It is the application of our belief that confirms who we truly are. You may remember that James went on to say, "faith without works is dead!"

There is an old saying, "the devil is in the details," which is true, but the reason he is in the details is to pervert them. His genius is counterfeiting. He counterfeits everything. He tries to make his ways look like God's ways so that we can hardly tell the difference. He is very clever. He has had thousands of years to practice and has been very successful. Without the help of the Holy Scripture and the Holy Spirit, we are no match for his deception.

We need to remember that the devil never created a single thing. God alone creates. The devil is by necessity a parasite, dependent solely on God's creation. He has to feed off of what God has created. He has to twist it, to mold and reshape it to make it serve his purpose. God created the details to bring truth and understanding, the devil specializes in corrupting everything that God created.

I decided to try a little trick on my friend. So I asked him, "How do you KNOW anything?" He thought I was trying to be a smart aleck and turned to walk away. But I stopped him. I said, "wait a minute, I'm serious, before you KNOW you are a Christian, shouldn't you KNOW how you came to KNOW what you think you KNOW? Isn't it fundamentally important to KNOW how you KNOW? What if the way you process information is all wrong? Or, what if the information you are processing is all wrong?"

He, like most people, was not interested in what philosophers call epistemology, or more practically, how we KNOW what we KNOW. Zombies and Kardashians are much more appealing to folks today than critical thinking skills. The general population is more content to live a lie than to take the time to chase the truth back to a fixed point. Some are convinced that the truth is too elusive, and a few self-appointed potentates openly declare that it does not exist.

I think we can safely say that human knowledge is acquired primarily by experience, or even more fundamentally, by faith in somebody else's experience. When Jesus showed Thomas the nail holes in his hands, Thomas received the experience he needed. Not having the necessary faith, he desired firsthand experience, which is the preferred method for most people. Seeing with his own eyes was the means by which Thomas came to believe that Jesus really did overcome death. But, we also know that even seeing is not necessarily believing, as most of the people who saw Jesus with their own eyes did not believe He was who He said He was.

Jesus fully realized that particular event was a moment in time the rest of us would never experience, that all people thereafter would require some other way of KNOWING. Therefore Jesus said, "blessed are those who have not seen but still believe." Jesus gives us permission to accept on faith what Thomas learned by experience. More often, faith is the only option.

However, our KNOWING by faith is as good as Thomas' KNOWING by experience. In fact, faith is superior to experience most of the time. For example, I do not have to stick my finger in a light socket to KNOW the results. I can accept on faith from some experienced authority that the results will be undesirable. It is the nature of truth to stubbornly exist, whether I believe it or not. In Thomas' case, the resurrection was already a reality before he accepted it as such. And, it would have remained a reality if he had continued to deny it.

Both faith and experience accumulate over the ages, handed down by one generation to the next. Whatever we think we KNOW, we KNOW because we have accepted it from some authority, or we have experienced it personally, or both. Often, faith in some revelation, or in someone else's experience, is the very thing that provokes us to act. And, quite often, this secondhand faith is not only the most consistent origin of human action but the only antidote for inaction.

Our actions then produce our own personal experience, which in turn proves the authenticity of our faith, thus perpetuating the cycle. Faith provokes action, action produces experience, experience affirms faith. This is fundamental, not only to living the Christian life, but to living any life that has meaning or purpose. Faith combined with works creates a living, growing, enduring faith.

When I observe the sun, I notice that it rises in the east and sets in the west. That has been my experience for nearly seven decades. I have faith now that it will repeat the process again tomorrow. Even when the clouds obscure the sun, I still know it is there. My ancestors tell me that their experience with the sun is identical to mine. My experience, combined with the accumulated experiences of my ancestors, has given me faith enough to say that I KNOW something. This gives me a fixed point from which to operate.

I KNOW that the sun rises in the east and sets in the west, and that belief is not affected by contrary opinions. People who think clearly know that absolutes exist and are never affected by contrary opinions. Nothing overrides established facts. Even the devil knows that. This is what we sometimes refer to as common sense. And the very reason common sense is not so common anymore is because people have been duped by the devil to believe that absolutes no longer exist, that everything is relative. If there were no absolutes then there would be no fixed point from which to operate. When there is no common place of origin, there is no common sense.

In respect to the sun rising and setting, my faith came like Thomas's, AFTER observing the fact.

On the other hand, what are we to think of Jesus' admonition, "blessed are those who have not observed the facts." (Powell translation)   If a mother tells her child that the stove is hot, you must not touch it. If the child has no experience with fire, acceptance of the mother's advice is the best option. If the child honors the mother's advice and accepts it on faith, a painful consequence may be avoided.

Avoiding a painful or disastrous consequence is the best argument for accepting things on faith. This is the very element that makes faith so profoundly superior to experience. There are many things that none of us want to learn by experience, not the least of which is the fires of hell.

The experience option, sometimes referred to as trial and error, is often followed by the phrase, "I told you so," demonstrating its inferiority by the fact that errors greatly outnumber successes. Children can KNOW that fire is dangerous, not because they have touched it, but because their mother told them so. In this case, their knowing comes before the experiential fact. Their faith-based knowledge came before they witnessed any evidence or action, making the trial and error system unnecessary. In most things, older generations are much more aware of consequences that younger generations rarely suspect. To the chagrin of the youngsters, this legitimizes that detestable adult response, "because I said so!"

My teacher told me that 2 + 2 = 4. I accepted it as a fact based on the authority of my teacher. I trusted my teacher. Most of what I KNOW I have accepted because somebody I trusted told me so. Fortunately, most of us had parents and teachers who told us the truth and we accepted it on faith, though some of us hard heads found it necessary to test some of it through experience. We are inclined to believe that people who love us the most do not want to hurt us by telling us a lie.

Unfortunately, we are finding that more people, even parents and teachers, are succumbing to the subtle influence of a perverted culture which renders them less trustworthy.

Consequently, more and more people in leadership positions mislead us; some because they are ignorant, or negligent; others because they are evil. The ignorant and negligent are more easily and most often misled by those who are truly evil. Massive and gross perversion and corruption is the ultimate condition of a godless society. Certainly, this makes the quest for truth more difficult, but much more a necessity.

Which brings me to a question even more critical than how we KNOW what we KNOW: The critical question is: "how do we distinguish a lie from the truth?" Since the object of our faith is the most critical component of all belief systems, the object of our faith must be trustworthy. This is the foundation upon which all truth must rest? To be reliable, statements must represent facts; they cannot rest on opinion, speculation, or perception. All lies are perversions of the truth. If truth did not exist, there would be no such thing as a lie. You can only identify a lie by comparing it to the truth.

We must have a fool proof way to identify liars, or false prophets, the "wolves in sheep's clothing," as Jesus called them. Contrary to what the secular elites tell us, perception is not reality. Whatever we believe should be grounded in reality. It has to have a history of consistency. It cannot contradict the wisdom accumulated through the ages. Not to discount unprecedented events, we must not believe the sun will come up in the west tomorrow morning.

We have to begin our quest for truth by engaging the self-proclaimed prophets. They must be exposed for what they are. We must be constantly curious. We must ask questions. Questions like: Is that person in authority a credible authority? Upon what evidence or authority do they base their claim? Does their claim contradict known realities? Have their previous predictions failed to materialize? Are they accustomed to making mistakes and miscalculations? Have they considered all the facts? Are they misinterpreting the facts? Do they play favorites with facts? Who, or what, is the source of their facts? What is their motive? Are they manipulating the facts to support a personal agenda?

In other words, the first step in finding truth is to challenge what is being presented as truth. Realizing it may be difficult cannot be a deterrent. We must not shy away from our own doubts. Lay all the cards on the table. In the American judicial system we have due process. We examine and cross examine. We challenge. We debate. We bring in witnesses and all the evidence we can muster. Then the jury goes in a back room and reconsiders it all over and over again.

Even then, there is no guarantee that they will arrive at the truth. Many of us have witnessed court cases that went on for weeks. When time for a verdict came, we still could not determine guilt or innocence. Some of us have sat on those juries. To avoid convicting an innocent person, we have built into our judicial system a number of safeguards: the presumption of innocence, Miranda rights, the requirement of proof beyond reasonable doubt, right to appeal… to mention a few.

However, we do know one thing—that the defendant is either guilty, or innocence, not both at the same time, for the same crime. We believe that the truth still exists even though we cannot presently identify it. We believe that there is at least one person in the courtroom who knows the truth. That is the fixed point from which we must always start.

Whenever we hear two totally different truth claims that blatantly contradict each other, we KNOW that both cannot be true. This law of non-contradiction is basic to finding what is true and what is false. The bottom line is — in all cases, truth exists, truth is absolute, and our ignorance of it does not affect its existence!

The questions then arise, "Where then is the ultimate credible source for all human knowledge?" Is there some way we can KNOW what we so desperately need to KNOW? Is there a process that goes beyond the normal means of KNOWING? If so, how do we employ it? I hope to answer these questions in the next few pages, but first I must identify a particular kind of truth, perhaps the most elementary kind of truth.

We should know by now that some truths are not necessarily immediately evident. In fact, many of us have come to expect a lie and a cover-up to precede the truth. We are really surprised when we meet an honest person. We have been lied to so much that we are skeptical of everything and everybody. We know that most of the time we will have to settle in and wait a while for the truth to emerge. We also know that time is one of our best friends when seeking the truth. Mark Twain once said, "a lie can race around the world while the truth is still tying its shoes."

Our forefathers were greatly concerned with truth as they began to lay the foundation for a new nation. They placed it up front in their vision statement: "We hold these truths to be self-evident that all men are created equal, that they are endowed by their Creator with certain unalienable Rights…"

In this short but powerful declaration, our forefathers imply at least five primary facts concerning truth: 1) truth originated with God, 2) human beings originated with God, 3) the idea of human rights originated with God, 4) the idea of equality originated with God, 5) without God there is no cause or reason for existence. The framers of the American Constitution considered these ideas as undeniable truths which effectively and purposefully anchor our national governance to the God of the Bible.

How could they so boldly declare all of their proposals to be self-evident? Did they KNOW something that most human beings do not KNOW? It is self-evident that the founders of our nation believed that a particular nation must choose between two forms of government. Either a nation will be governed by the Grace of a particular God, or by the tyranny of particular men. It is also self-evident as to their preference.

Now to the question of whether there is an alternative way of receiving knowledge that exists outside the norm of authority and experience. The apostle Paul addressed this issue at various times during his ministry. In his letter to the Romans he enlightens us with these words: "The wrath of God is being revealed from heaven against all the godlessness and wickedness of men who suppress the truth by their wickedness, since what may be known about God is plain to them, because God has made it plain to them. For since the creation of the world God's invisible qualities—his eternal powers and divine nature—have been clearly seen, being understood from what has been made, so that men are without excuse. For although they knew God, they neither glorified him as God nor gave thanks to him, but their thinking became futile and their foolish hearts were darkened. Although they claimed to be wise, they became fools and exchanged the glory of the immortal God for images made to look like mortal man and birds and animals and reptiles." (Romans 1:18-23 NIV)

The clue that Paul is revealing is that human beings have been hard wired even before birth to know certain things instinctively. We have, as William James says, "a faculty of acting in such a way as to produce certain ends, without foresight of the ends, and without previous education in the performance." A bird does not take a course in nest building, or hatching eggs, or flying south in the winter. A bird is born knowing these things. Likewise, humans are instilled with an instinctive knowledge of God. A man who says there is no God is like a bird who has decided to no longer build nests, hatch eggs, and fly south. The Bible says that such a bird, or such a man, is a fool.

C.S. Lewis takes the next step, "Creatures are not born with desires unless satisfaction for those desires exists. A baby feels hunger: well, there is such a thing as food. A duckling wants to swim: well, there is such a thing as water. Men feel sexual desire: well, there is such a thing as sex. If I find in myself a desire which no experience in this world can satisfy, the most probable explanation is that I was made for another world." Included in God's engineering design for mankind is our instinctive ability to embrace the concept of Eternity.

Paul continues to pursue this other way of knowing: "However, as it is written: 'No eye has seen, nor ear has heard, no mind has conceived what God has prepared for those who love him' – but God has revealed to us by his Spirit. The Spirit searches all things, even the deep things of God. For who among men knows the thoughts of a man except the man's spirit within him? In the same way no one knows the thoughts of God except the Spirit of God. We have not received the spirit of the world but the Spirit who is from God, that we may understand what God has freely given us. This is what we speak, not in words taught us by human wisdom, but in words taught by the Spirit, expressing spiritual truths in spiritual words. The man without the Spirit does not accept the things that come from the Spirit of God, for they are foolishness to him, and he cannot understand them, because they are spiritually discerned. The spiritual man makes judgments about all things, but he himself is not subject to any man's judgment: 'For who has known the mind of the Lord that he may instruct him?' But we have the mind of Christ." (1 Corinthians 2:9-16 NIV)

Paul then summarizes for us why God created an alternative way of communicating that exists above and beyond our five senses: "For our struggle is not against flesh and blood, but against the rulers, against the authorities, against the powers of this dark world and against the spiritual forces of evil in the heavenly realms." (Ephesians 6:12 NIV)

One of the dominate concerns of the disciples and the early church leaders was the prevalence of false teachers. They seemed to fall into two groups---those who misinterpret God's Word out of ignorance, and those who distort it out of malice. People who are honestly ignorant can be easily corrected, but that is not the case with the dishonest. Throughout the Bible we find severe warnings issued to those who willfully and purposefully distort God's Word. Christians today should pay close attention to these warnings.

Jude describes false teachers this way: "For certain men have secretly slipped in among you. They are godless men, who change the grace of our God into a license for immorality and deny Jesus Christ our only Sovereign and Lord...woe to them! They have taken the way of Cain; they have rushed for profit into Balaam's error, they have been destroyed in Korah's rebellion. These men are blemishes at your love feast, eating with you without slightest qualm—shepherds who feed only themselves. They are clouds without rain, blown along by the wind; autumn trees, without fruit and uprooted—twice dead. They are wild waves of the sea, foaming up their shame, wandering stars, for whom blackest darkness has been reserved forever... these men are grumblers and faultfinders; they follow their own evil desires; they boast about themselves and flatter others for their own advantage...these are the men who divide you, who follow mere natural instincts and do not have the Spirit." (Jude 4, 12, 13, 16, 19 NIV)

The apostle John adds his warning: "Dear Children, do not let anyone lead you astray. He who does what is right is righteous, just as he is righteous. He who does what is sinful is of the devil, because the devil has been sinning from the beginning. The reason the Son of God appeared was to destroy the devil's work. No one who is born of God will continue in sin because God's seed remains in him; he cannot go on sinning because he has been born of God. This is how we know who the children of God are and who the children of the devil are: Anyone who does not do what is right is not a child of God; nor is anyone who does not love his brother...Dear friends, do not believe every spirit, but test the spirits to see whether they are from God, because many false prophets have gone out into the world. This is how you can recognize the Spirit of God: Every spirit that acknowledges that Jesus Christ has come in the flesh is from God, but every spirit that does not acknowledge Jesus is not from God. (1 John 3: 7-10, 4: 1-3 NIV)

Paul cautioned two young preachers in this way: "Avoid godless chatter because those who indulge in it will become more and more ungodly. Their teaching will spread like gangrene. Among them are Hymenaeus and Philetus who have wandered away from the truth." (2 Timothy 2:16-17 NIV) "For there are many rebellious people, mere talkers, and deceivers, especially those of the circumcision group. They must be silenced, because they are ruining whole households by teaching things they ought not to teach—and that for the sake of dishonest gain." (Titus 1: 10-11 NIV)

Peter had dealings with false teachers as well: "But there were also false prophets among the people, just as there will be false prophets among you. They will secretly introduce destructive heresies, even denying the sovereign Lord who bought them—bringing swift destruction on themselves. Many will follow their shameful ways and will bring the way of truth into disrepute. In their greed these teachers will exploit you with stories they have made up…these men are springs without water and mists driven by a storm. Blackest darkness is reserved for them. For they mouth empty, boastful words and by appealing to the lustful desires of sinful human nature, they entice people who are just escaping from those who live in error. They promise them freedom, while they themselves are slaves of depravity—for a man is a slave to whatever has mastered him… Of them the proverbs are true" 'A dog returns to its vomit,' and, 'a sow that is washed goes back to her wallowing in the mud.'" (2 Peter 2: 1-3, 17-19, 22 NIV)

Jesus was the one most aware of false prophets. He issued the most comprehensive warning: "Watch out for false prophets. They come to you in sheep's clothing, but inwardly they are ferocious wolves. By their fruit you will recognize them. Do people pick grapes from thorn bushes, or figs from thistles? Likewise every good tree bears good fruit, but every bad tree bears bad fruit. A good tree cannot bear bad fruit, and a bad tree cannot bear good fruit. Every tree that does not bear good fruit is cut down and thrown into the fire. Thus, by their fruit you will recognize them. Not everyone who says to me, 'Lord, Lord,' will enter the kingdom of heaven, but only he who does the will of my Father who is in heaven. Many will say to me on that day, 'Lord, Lord, did we not prophesy in your name, and in your name drive out demons and perform many miracles?' Then I will tell them plainly, 'I never knew you, Away from me, you evil doers!'" (Matthew 7: 15-23 NIV)

Who are the false teachers today? They are the ones who attempt to secularize the church. In 2007, Dinesh D'Souza authored a book entitled, "What's So Great About Christianity." He unveiled an interesting paradox. He stated, "If secularization were proceeding inexorably, then religious people should be getting less religious, and so conservative churches should be shrinking and liberal churches growing. In fact, the opposite is the case.

Using statistics compiled by the Institute of Religion and Democracy (2005), D'Souza reports, "In 1960, the Presbyterian Church had 4.2 million members; now it has 2.4 million. The Episcopal Church had 3.4 million members; now it has 2.3 million. The United Church of Christ had 2.2 million members; now it has 1.3 million. The churches affiliated with the Southern Baptist Convention had 8.7 million members; now they have 16.4 million."

Why the disparity? According to D'Souza, "the traditional Christians who remained within liberal churches became increasingly alienated." A traditional Christian will not remain in a church that mimics the ways of the world. A true Christian will not compromise the authority and the integrity of the Bible to make the message more attractive to the culture.

Liberal interpreters of the Bible attempt to reverse the very mission of the church, as D'Souza cleverly surmises, "instead of being the church's missionaries to the world, they have become the world's missionaries to the church. They devote their moral energies to trying to make the church more democratic, to assure equal rights for women, to legitimize homosexual marriage, and so on." The secularist are not content to kick Jesus out of the public square, they desire to kick Him out of His own church!

It is easy for Christians in America to see that we are under relentless attack. Satan, the roaring lion he is, will take the easy prey first, the weak and the young. The most pressing need for spiritually mature Christians is to protect and shelter the weak and young among us and help them to grow up fast. We need fathers to become the spiritual leaders of their homes, we need role models and mentors on every street corner. We need prayer warriors from wall to wall. We need an army. Come join us!

Epilogue

Winston Churchill said, "Writing a book is an adventure. To begin with it is a toy and an amusement. Then it becomes a mistress, then it becomes a master, then it becomes a tyrant. The last phase is that as you are about to be reconciled to your servitude, you kill the monster and fling him to the public."

Now that the thing is dead there is no reason for me to mourn over those things I wish I had said, or said better. In the final days, I tried to go back and edit, but it became a more hideous monster, so I left it alone. For now, it is what it is.

Since I dedicated this writing to my grandchildren, and yours, the very best that can come out of it is for one of them to say, "Yah Yah helped me to understand who Jesus really is…"

Appendix

*Letters to an atheist:

Dear Friend,

Our conversation on last Tuesday was enlightening but troubling. You seemed very content and confident in your belief that death is the end, that nothing occurs in the world of the dead afterwards, that there is no such thing as eternal life, heaven, or hell, or anything else.

You appeared to be convinced that mankind originated through a process of evolution over the course of billions of years of random upgrades. You acknowledged several selected scientific discoveries to support your belief. I desire to know more about the foundation on which you build your belief system. Perhaps I have missed certain critical pieces of information which would disqualify me from further comment.

My experience with the evolution theory as a vehicle to transport us back to the beginning is one of constant breakdown. It only transports me downhill, through various changes within a species. It is pretty dependable transportation through these local, short, downhill sprints. But, I cannot get it to go uphill, particularly when I try to cross the three steep bridges from 1) nothing to something, 2) from something to life, 3) from life to man. It stubbornly sits forever motionless at the bottom of each bridge.

A true and honest scientist will acknowledge the fallibility of science in general, and more specifically its limited capacity to provide explanations for human origins. The value of science is in explaining how the universe works, not how it got here.

It would be unfair for me to inject the design theory at this point since the design theory is not earth bound, as scientific theories are, and, as you say, an easy out. I prefer instead to get a running start and see if we can get that old worn out jalopy of yours up and over any of the three bridges that stand in its way. Then, we will have a vehicle with a little trade-in value.

In the mean time, I paraphrase the great scientist, Pascal, who wagers the following: If I believe in heaven and hell and you do not, and it turns out that you are right, then, no consequence awaits us. But, if it turns out that I am right, there is a most definite consequence to greet us both.

I am not a poker player, at least not lately, but if I were, I would make the safe bet. It is beyond dangerous for us to miscalculate on something as critical as eternal life, especially when our decision affects the decisions of others. All of life's decisions pale in significance to this one. Think long and hard about it…

Your friend,

tp

Dear Friend,

Conversations with you encourage me to publish the memoirs of my hallowed and humorous quest for truth. In my search for answers, I remember asking myself, "how will I recognize the truth if I find it?" I recall a second question of a more weighty significance, "If I recognize it, will I be willing to accept it?"

With the multiplicity of ideas and opinions, there must be some formula by which we can distinguish fact from fiction. With the secret motive of every man to retail his personal bias as the wholesale truth, how do we ever avoid the whims and flaws that constantly afflict the nature of man? Who do we trust? Is science the gold standard by which every idea must live or die? Can science stand in judgment of that which it has not yet discovered? Who is accountable for its mistakes?

Science, as we know it today, is bound up in the mind of man and is confined to and dependent upon man's accumulated knowledge. Science is exploratory in nature and progresses through trial and error, constantly replacing old ideas with new ones. What we know now we learned from the mistakes of the past, what we will know in the future, we will hopefully learn from our present mistakes.

The relative nature of science makes it an inferior and fallible instrument for measuring truth. Simply stated, truth is always there before science discovers it. The forte of science is always after the fact, and often, centuries after the fact. What science can test and measure it can confirm. But, germs existed before science picked up on the clue that cleanliness is next to godliness.

The scientific principles which provide the foundation for modern technology have always existed. The planet earth has always been circular, even when scientist thought otherwise. This kind of preexistence is forever outside the scope of science. Science at best can affirm what exists at any given time, and through additional time and effort and manmade tools uncover that which already exists.

The critical difference in the Design theory and the evolutionary theory is the inherent inequality in capacity. Only that which exists eternally can explain eternal existence. The Designer can, from the onset, or at any point in time, perfectly explain everything because, having created it, He exists independent of it. Furthermore, He is accountable for it, and true to it–a couple of notions of which science is negligent.

I will ride around town with you in yo old broke down Darwinian vehicle, but I ain't getting out of the interstate with it.

Your friend,

tp